The Psychic Life of Power

Theories in Subjection

The
Psychic Life
of Power

Theories in Subjection

■

Judith Butler

Stanford University Press
Stanford, California

Stanford University Press
Stanford, California
© 1997 by the Board of Trustees of the
Leland Stanford Junior University

Printed in the United States of America

CIP data appear at the end of the book

Acknowledgments

This work was generously sponsored by a Humanities Research Fellowship from the University of California at Berkeley. I am grateful to those friends and colleagues who gave incisive readings of some of the chapters: Wendy Brown, William Connolly, David Palumbo-Liu, Kaja Silverman, Anne Norton, Denise Riley, and Hayden White, as well as the students who participated in "Social Subjects / Psychic States" at Berkeley. I thank Adam Phillips for his permission to reprint our exchange from *Psychoanalytic Dialogues* in this context. I also thank Helen Tartar for her meticulous, intelligent, and thoroughgoing editing, and Gayle Salamon for her assistance with the manuscript.

Contents

The Psychic Life of Power

Theories in Subjection

Introduction

We should try to grasp subjection in its material instance as
a constitution of subjects.

> —Michel Foucault, "Two Lectures"

The splitting of the subject, within which the self as present
to itself is only one moment, and the charged reflexivity of
that moment, is the point of purchase within the subject of
its subjection. The profound and corporeal guilt with which
the subject is invested as the febrile undertone of that self-
consciousness, which turns out to know so little of itself, is
decisive in securing the deep inner control, which has been
called interpellation.

> —Francis Barker, *The Tremulous Private Body:
> Essays on Subjection*

Subjection . . . The act or fact of being subjected, as under a
monarch or other sovereign or superior power; the state of
being subject to, or under the dominion of another; hence
gen. subordination. . . . The condition of being subject,
exposed, or liable *to*; liability. . . . *Logic.* The act of supplying
a subject to a predicate.   —*Oxford English Dictionary*

As a form of power, subjection is paradoxical. To be domi-
nated by a power external to oneself is a familiar and
agonizing form power takes. To find, however, that what "one"

is, one's very formation as a subject, is in some sense dependent upon that very power is quite another. We are used to thinking of power as what presses on the subject from the outside, as what subordinates, sets underneath, and relegates to a lower order. This is surely a fair description of part of what power does. But if, following Foucault, we understand power as *forming* the subject as well, as providing the very condition of its existence and the trajectory of its desire, then power is not simply what we oppose but also, in a strong sense, what we depend on for our existence and what we harbor and preserve in the beings that we are. The customary model for understanding this process goes as follows: power imposes itself on us, and, weakened by its force, we come to internalize or accept its terms. What such an account fails to note, however, is that the "we" who accept such terms are fundamentally dependent on those terms for "our" existence. Are there not discursive conditions for the articulation of any "we"? Subjection consists precisely in this fundamental dependency on a discourse we never chose but that, paradoxically, initiates and sustains our agency.

"Subjection" signifies the process of becoming subordinated by power as well as the process of becoming a subject. Whether by interpellation, in Althusser's sense, or by discursive productivity, in Foucault's, the subject is initiated through a primary submission to power. Although Foucault identifies the ambivalence in this formulation, he does not elaborate on the specific mechanisms of how the subject is formed in submission. Not only does the entire domain of the psyche remain largely unremarked in his theory, but power in this double valence of subordinating and producing remains unexplored. Thus, if submission is a condition of subjection, it makes sense to ask: What is the psychic form that power takes? Such a project requires thinking the theory of power together with a theory of the psyche, a task that has been eschewed by writers in both Foucauldian and psychoanalytic orthodoxies. Though it offers no promise of a grand synthesis, the present inquiry seeks to explore the provisional perspectives from which each theory illuminates the other. The project neither begins nor ends with Freud and Foucault; the question of subjection, of how the subject is formed in subordination, preoccupies the section of Hegel's *Phenomenology of Spirit* that traces the slave's approach to freedom and his disappointing fall into the "unhappy consciousness." The master, who at first appears to be "external" to the slave, reemerges as the slave's own conscience. The unhappiness of the consciousness that emerges is its own self-beratement, the effect of the transmutation of the master into a psychic reality. The self-mortifications that seek to redress the insistent corporeality of self-consciousness institute bad conscience. This figure of consciousness turned back upon itself prefigures Nietzsche's account, in *On the Genealogy of Morals*, not only of how repression and regulation form the overlapping phenomena of conscience and bad conscience, but also of how the latter become essential to the formation, persistence, and continuity of the subject. In each case, power that at first appears as external, pressed upon the subject, pressing the subject into subordination, assumes a psychic form that constitutes the subject's self-identity.

The form this power takes is relentlessly marked by a figure of turning, a turning back upon oneself or even a turning *on* oneself. This figure operates as part of the explanation of how a subject is produced, and so there is no subject, strictly speaking, who makes this turn. On the contrary, the turn appears to function as a tropological inauguration of the subject, a founding moment whose ontological status remains permanently uncertain. Such a notion, then, appears difficult, if not impossible, to incorporate into the account of subject formation. What or who is said to turn, and what is the object of such a turn? How is it that a subject is wrought from such an ontologically uncertain form of twisting? Perhaps with the advent of this figure, we are no longer in the business of "giving an account of the formation of the subject." We are, rather, confronted with the tropological presumption made by any such explanation, one that facilitates the explanation but also marks its limit. The moment we seek to determine how power produces its subject, how the subject takes in the power by which it is inaugurated, we seem to enter this tropological quandary. We cannot presume a subject who performs an internalization if the formation of the subject is in need of explanation. The figure to which we refer has not yet acquired existence and is not part of a verifiable explanation, yet our reference continues to make a certain kind of sense. The paradox of subjection implies a paradox of referentiality: namely, that we must refer to what does not yet exist. Through a figure that marks the suspension of our ontological commitments, we seek to account for how the subject comes to be. That this figure is itself a "turn" is, rhetorically, performatively spectacular; "turn" translates the Greek sense of "trope." Thus the trope of the turn both indicates and exemplifies the tropological status of the gesture.[1] Does subjection inaugurate tropology in some way, or is the inaugurative work of tropes necessarily invoked when we try to account for the generation of the subject? We will return to this question toward the end of this inquiry when we consider how the explanation of melancholia participates in the mechanism it describes, producing psychic topographies that are clearly tropological.

The scene of "interpellation" offered by Althusser is one

instance of this quasi-fictive effort to give an account of how the social subject is produced through linguistic means. Althusser's doctrine of interpellation clearly sets the stage for Foucault's later views on the "discursive production of the subject." Foucault, of course, insists that the subject is not "spoken" into existence and that the matrices of power and discourse that constitute the subject are neither singular nor sovereign in their productive action. Yet Althusser and Foucault agree that there is a founding subordination in the process of *assujetissement*. In Althusser's essay "Ideology and Ideological State Apparatuses," the subordination of the subject takes place through language, as the effect of the authoritative voice that hails the individual. In the infamous example that Althusser offers, a policeman hails a passerby on the street, and the passerby turns and recognizes himself as the one who is hailed. In the exchange by which that recognition is proferred and accepted, interpellation—the discursive production of the social subject—takes place. Significantly, Althusser does not offer a clue as to why that individual turns around, accepting the voice as being addressed to him or her, and accepting the subordination and normalization effected by that voice. Why does this subject turn toward the voice of the law, and what is the effect of such a turn in inaugurating a social subject? Is this a guilty subject and, if so, how did it become guilty? Might the theory of interpellation require a theory of conscience?

The interpellation of the subject through the inaugurative address of state authority presupposes not only that the inculcation of conscience already has taken place, but that conscience, understood as the psychic operation of a regulatory norm, constitutes a specifically psychic and social working of power on which interpellation depends but for which it can give no account. Moreover, the model of power in Althusser's account attributes performative power to the authoritative voice, the voice of sanction, and hence to a notion of language figured as speech. How are we to account for the power of written discourse, or of bureaucratic discourse, which circulates without voice or signature? Finally, Althusser's view, useful as it is, remains implicitly constrained by a notion of a centralized state apparatus, one whose word is its deed, modeled on divine authority. The notion of discourse emerges in Foucault in part to counter the sovereign model of interpellative speech in theories such as Althusser's, but also to take account of the *efficacy* of discourse apart from its instantiation as the spoken word.

Passionate Attachments

The insistence that a subject is passionately attached to his or her own subordination has been invoked cynically by those who seek to debunk the claims of the subordinated. If a subject can be shown to pursue or sustain his or her subordinated status, the reasoning goes, then perhaps final responsibility for that subordination resides with the subject. Over and against this view, I would maintain that the attachment to subjection is produced through the workings of power, and that part of the operation of power is made clear in this psychic effect, one of the most insidious of its productions If, in a Nietzschean sense, the subject is formed by a will that turns back upon itself, assuming a reflexive form, then the subject is the modality of power that turns on itself; the subject is the effect of power in recoil. ❘ response q Power

The subject who is at once formed and subordinated is already implicated in the scene of psychoanalysis. Foucault's reformulation of subordination as that which is not only pressed on a subject but forms a subject, that is, is pressed on a subject by its formation, suggests an ambivalence at the site where the subject emerges. If the effect of autonomy is conditioned by subordination and that founding subordination or dependency is rigorously repressed, the subject emerges in tandem with the unconscious. The Foucaultian postulation of subjection as the simultaneous subordination and forming of the subject assumes a specific psychoanalytic valence when we consider that no subject emerges without a passionate attachment to those on whom he or she is fundamentally dependent (even if that passion is "negative" in the psychoanalytic sense). Although the dependency of the child is not *political* subordination in any usual sense, the formation of primary passion in dependency renders the child vulnerable to subordination and exploitation, a topic that has become a preoccupation of recent political discourse. Moreover, this situation of primary dependency conditions the political formation and regulation of subjects and becomes the means of their subjection. If there is no formation of the subject without a passionate attachment to those by whom she or he is subordinated, then subordination proves central to the becoming of the subject.[2] As the condition of becoming a subject, subordination implies being in a mandatory submission. Moreover, the desire to survive, "to be," is a pervasively exploitable desire. The one who holds out the promise of continued existence plays to the desire to survive. "I would rather exist in subordination than not exist" is one formulation of this predicament (where the risk of "death" is also possible). This is one reason why debates about the reality of the sexual abuse of children tend to misstate the character of the exploitation. It is not simply that a sexuality is unilaterally imposed by the adult, nor that a sexuality is unilaterally fantasized by the child, but that the child's love, a love that is necessary for its existence, is exploited and a passionate attachment abused.

Let us consider that a subject is not only formed in subordination, but that this subordination provides the subject's continuing condition of possibility. A child's love is prior to judgment and decision; a child tended and nourished in a "good enough" way will love, and only later stand a chance of discriminating among those he or she loves. This is to say, not that the child loves blindly (since from early on there is discernment and "knowingness" of an important kind), but only that if the child is to persist in a psychic and social sense, there must be dependency and the formation of attachment: there is no possibility of not loving, where love is bound up with the requirements for life. The child does not know to what he/she attaches; yet the infant as well as the child must attach in order to persist in and as itself.[3] No subject can emerge without this attachment, formed in dependency, but no subject, in the course of its formation, can ever afford fully to "see" it. This attachment in its primary forms must both *come to be* and *be denied*, its coming to be must consist in its partial denial, for the subject to emerge.

That accounts in part for the adult sense of humiliation when confronted with the earliest objects of love—parents, guardians, siblings, and so on—the sense of belated indignation in which one claims, "I couldn't possibly love such a person." The utterance concedes the possibility it denies, establishing the "I" as predicated upon that foreclosure, grounded in and by that firmly imagined impossibility. The "I" is thus fundamentally threatened by the specter of this (impossible) love's reappearance and remains condemned to reenact that love unconsciously, repeatedly reliving and displacing that scandal, that impossibility, orchestrating that threat to one's sense of "I." " 'I' could not be who I am if I were to love in the way that I apparently did, which I must, to persist as myself, continue to deny and yet unconsciously reenact in contemporary life with the most terrible suffering as its consequence." The traumatic repetition of what has been foreclosed from contemporary life threatens the "I." Through that neurotic repetition the subject pursues its own dissolution, its own unraveling, a pursuit that marks an agency, but not the *subject's* agency—rather, the agency of a desire that aims at the dissolution of the subject, where the subject stands as a bar to that desire.[4]

If the subject is produced through foreclosure, then the subject is produced by a condition from which it is, by definition, separated and differentiated. Desire will aim at unraveling the subject, but be thwarted by precisely the subject in whose name it operates. A vexation of desire, one that proves crucial to subjection, implies that for the subject to persist, the subject must thwart its own desire. And for desire to triumph, the subject must be threatened with dissolution. A subject turned against itself (its desire) appears, on this model, to be a condition of the persistence of the subject.

To desire the conditions of one's own subordination is thus required to persist as oneself. What does it mean to embrace the very form of power—regulation, prohibition, suppression —that threatens one with dissolution in an effort, precisely, to persist in one's own existence? It is not simply that one requires the recognition of the other and that a form of recognition is conferred through subordination, but rather that one is dependent on power for one's very formation, that that formation is impossible without dependency, and that the posture of the adult subject consists precisely in the denial and reenactment of this dependency. The "I" emerges upon the condition that it deny its formation in dependency, the conditions of its own possibility. The "I," however, is threatened with disruption precisely by this denial, by its unconscious pursuit of its own dissolution through neurotic repetitions that restage the primary scenarios it not only refuses to see but cannot see, if it wishes to remain itself. This means, of course, that, predicated on what it refuses to know, it is separated from itself and can never quite become or remain itself.

Ambivalence

The notion of the subject has incited controversy within recent theoretical debate, being promoted by some as a necessary precondition of agency and reviled by others as a sign of "mastery" to be refused. My purpose is neither to enumerate nor to resolve the contemporary instances of this debate. Rather, I propose to take account of how a paradox recurrently structures the debate, leading it almost always to culminate in displays of ambivalence How can it be that the subject, taken to be the condition for and instrument of agency, is at the same time the effect of subordination, understood as the deprivation of agency? If subordination is the condition of possibility for agency, how might agency be thought in opposition to the forces of subordination?

"The subject" is sometimes bandied about as if it were interchangeable with "the person" or "the individual." The genealogy of the subject as a critical category, however, suggests that the subject, rather than be identified strictly with the individual, ought to be designated as a linguistic category, a placeholder, a structure in formation. Individuals come to occupy the site of the subject (the subject simultaneously emerges as a "site"), and they enjoy intelligibility only to the extent that they are, as it were, first established in language. The subject is the linguistic occasion for the individual to achieve and reproduce intelligibility, the linguistic condition of its existence and agency. No individual becomes a subject without first becoming subjected or undergoing "subjectivation" (a translation of the French *assujetissement*). It makes little sense to treat "the individual" as an intelligible term if individuals are said to acquire their intelligibility by becoming subjects. Paradoxically, no intelligible reference to individuals or their becoming can take place without a prior reference to their status as subjects. The story by which subjection is told is, inevitably, circular, presupposing the very subject for which it seeks to give an account. On the one hand, the subject can refer to its own genesis only by taking a third-person perspective on itself, that is, by dispossessing its own perspective in the act of narrating its genesis. On the other hand, the narration of how the subject is constituted presupposes that the constitution has already taken place, and thus arrives after the fact. The subject loses itself to tell the story of itself, but in telling the story of itself seeks to give an account of what the narrative function has already made plain. What does it mean, then, that the subject, defended by some as a presupposition of agency, is also understood to be an *effect* of subjection? Such a formulation suggests that in the act of opposing subordination, the subject reiterates its subjection (a notion shared by both psychoanalysis and Foucauldian accounts). How, then, is subjection to be thought and how can it become a site of alteration? A power *exerted on* a subject, subjection is nevertheless a power *assumed by* the subject, an assumption that constitutes the instrument of that subject's becoming.

Subjection/Subordination

The double aspect of subjection appears to lead to a vicious circle: the agency of the subject appears to be an effect of its subordination. Any effort to oppose that subordination will necessarily presuppose and reinvoke it. Luckily, the story survives this impasse. What does it mean for the agency of a subject to *presuppose* its own subordination? Is the act of *presupposing* the same as the act of *reinstating*, or is there a discontinuity between the power presupposed and the power reinstated? Consider that in the very act by which the subject reproduces the conditions of its own subordination, the subject exemplifies a temporally based vulnerability that belongs to those conditions, specifically, to the exigencies of their renewal. Power considered as a condition of the subject is necessarily not the same as power considered as what the subject is said to wield. The power that initiates the subject fails to remain continuous with the power that is the subject's agency. A significant and potentially enabling reversal occurs when power shifts from its status as a condition of agency to the subject's "own" agency (constituting an appearance of power in which the subject appears as the condition of its "own" power). How are we to assess that becoming? Is it an enabling break, a bad break? How is it that the power upon which the subject depends for existence and which the subject is compelled to reiterate turns against itself in the course of that reiteration? How might we think resistance within the terms of reiteration?

Such a view suggests that agency cannot logically be derived from its conditions, that no continuity is to be assumed between (a) what makes power possible and (b) the kinds of possibilities that power assumes. If in acting the subject retains the conditions of its emergence, this does not imply that all of its agency remains tethered to those conditions and that those conditions remain the same in every operation of agency. Assuming power is not a straightforward task of taking power from one place, transferring it intact, and then and there making it one's own; the act of appropriation may involve an alteration of power such that the power assumed or appropriated works against the power that made that assumption possible. Where conditions of subordination make possible the assumption of power, the power assumed remains tied to those conditions, but in an ambivalent way; in fact, the power assumed may at once retain and resist that subordination. This conclusion is not to be thought of as (a) a resistance that is *really* a recuperation of power or (b) a recuperation that is *really* a resistance. It is both at once, and this ambivalence forms the bind of agency.

According to the formulation of subjection as both the subordination and becoming of the subject, power is, as subordination, a set of conditions that precedes the subject, effecting and subordinating the subject from the outside. This formulation falters, however, when we consider that there is no subject prior to this effect. Power not only *acts on* a subject but, in a transitive sense, *enacts* the subject into being. As a condition, power precedes the subject. Power loses its appearance of priority, however, when it is wielded by the subject, a situation that gives rise to the reverse perspective that power is the effect of the subject, and that power is what subjects effect. A condition does not enable or enact without becoming present. Because Power is not intact prior to the subject, the appearance of its priority disappears as power acts on the subject, and the subject is inaugurated (and derived) through this tem-

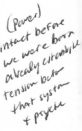

(Power)
intact before
we were born
already established
tension btw
that system
+ psyche

poral reversal in the horizon of power. As the agency of the subject, power assumes its present temporal dimension.[5]

Power acts on the subject in at least two ways: first, as what makes the subject possible, the condition of its possibility and its formative occasion, and second, as what is taken up and reiterated in the subject's "own" acting. As a subject *of* power (where "of" connotes both "belonging to" and "wielding"), the subject eclipses the conditions of its own emergence; it eclipses power with power. The conditions not only make possible the subject but enter into the subject's formation. They are made present in the acts of that formation and in the acts of the subject that follow.

The notion of power at work in subjection thus appears in two incommensurable temporal modalities: first, as what is for the subject always prior, outside of itself, and operative from the start; second, as the willed effect of the subject. This second modality carries at least two sets of meanings: as the willed effect of the subject, subjection is a subordination that the subject brings on itself; yet if subjection produces a subject and a subject is the precondition of agency, then subjection is the account by which a subject becomes the guarantor of its resistance and opposition. Whether power is conceived as prior to the subject or as its instrumental effect, the vacillation between the two temporal modalities of power ("before" and "after" the subject) has marked most of the debates on the subject and the problem of agency. Many conversations on the topic have become mired in whether the subject is the condition or the impasse of agency. Indeed, both quandaries have led many to consider the issue of the subject as an inevitable stumbling block in social theory. Part of this difficulty, I suggest, is that the subject is itself a site of this ambivalence in which the subject emerges both as the *effect* of a prior power and as the *condition of possibility* for a radically conditioned form of agency. A theory of the subject should take into account the full ambivalence of the conditions of its operation.

There is, as it were, no conceptual transition to be made between power as external to the subject, "acting on," and power as constitutive of the subject, "acted by." What one might expect by way of a transition is, in fact, a splitting and reversal constitutive of the subject itself. Power acts on the subject, an acting that is an enacting: an irresolvable ambiguity arises when one attempts to distinguish between the power that (transitively) enacts the subject, and the power enacted by the subject, that is, between the power that forms the subject and the subject's "own" power. What or who is doing the "enacting" here? Is it a power prior to the subject or that of the subject itself? At some point, a reversal and concealment occurs, and power emerges as what belongs exclusively to the subject (making the subject appear as if it belonged to no prior operation of power). Moreover, what is enacted by the subject is enabled but not finally constrained by the prior working of power. Agency exceeds the power by which it is enabled. One might say that the purposes of power are not always the purposes of agency. To the extent that the latter diverge from the former, agency is the assumption of a purpose *unintended* by power, one that could not have been derived logically or historically, that operates in a relation of contingency and reversal to the power that makes it possible, to which it nevertheless belongs. This is, as it were, the ambivalent scene of agency, constrained by no teleological necessity.

Power is both external to the subject and the very venue of the subject. This apparent contradiction makes sense when we understand that no subject comes into being without power, but that its coming into being involves the dissimulation of power, a metaleptic reversal in which the subject produced by power becomes heralded as the subject who *founds* power. This foundationalism of the subject is an effect of a working of power, an effect achieved by reversal and concealment of that prior working. This does not mean that the subject can be *reduced* to the power by which it is occasioned, nor does it mean that the power by which it is occasioned is *reducible to* the subject. Power is never merely a condition external or prior to the subject, nor can it be exclusively identified with the subject. If conditions of power are to persist, they must be reiterated; the subject is precisely the site of such reiteration, a repetition that is never merely mechanical. As the appearance of power shifts from the condition of the subject to its effects, the conditions of power (prior and external) assume a present and futural form. But power assumes this present character through a reversal of its direction, one that performs a break with what has come before and dissimulates as a self-inaugurating agency. The reiteration of power not only temporalizes the conditions of subordination but shows these conditions to be, not static structures, but temporalized—active and productive. The temporalization performed by reiteration traces the route by which power's appearance shifts and reverses: the perspective of power alters from what is always working on us from the outside and from the outset to what constitutes the sense of agency at work in our present acts and the futural expanse of their effects.

Although this study is indebted to Foucault's formulation of the problem of *assujetissement* in his essays "The Subject of Power" and the "Two Lectures" published in *Power/Knowledge*, as well as to his many discussions of the subject of desire and the subject of law in *History of Sexuality, Volumes 1 and 2* and *Discipline and Punish*,[6] the formulation of the subject at issue resonates with a larger cultural and political predicament, namely, how to take an oppositional relation to power that is, admittedly, implicated in the very power one opposes. Often this postliberatory insight has led to the conclusion that all agency here meets its impasse. Either forms of capital or symbolic domination are held to be such that our acts are always already "domesticated" in advance, or a set of generalized and timeless insights is offered into the aporetic structure of all movements toward a future. I would suggest that no historical or logical conclusions follow necessarily from this primary complicity with subordination, but that some possibilities tentatively do. That agency is implicated in subordination is not the sign of a fatal self-contradiction at the core of the subject and, hence, further proof of its pernicious or obsolete character. But neither does it restore a pristine notion of the subject, derived from some classical liberal-humanist formulation, whose agency is always and only opposed to power. The first view characterizes politically sanctimonious forms of fatalism; the second, naive forms of political optimism. I hope to steer clear of both these alternatives.

The subject might yet be thought as deriving its agency from precisely the power it opposes, as awkward and embarrassing as such a formulation might be, especially for those who believe that complicity and ambivalence could be rooted out once and for all. If the subject is *neither* fully determined by power *nor* fully determining of power (but significantly and partially both), the subject exceeds the logic of noncontradiction, is an excrescence of logic, as it were.[7] To claim that the subject exceeds either/or is not to claim that it lives in some free zone of its own making. Exceeding is not escaping, and the subject exceeds precisely that to which it is bound. In this sense, the subject cannot quell the ambivalence by which it is constituted. Painful, dynamic, and promising, this vacillation between the already-there and the yet-to-come is a crossroads that rejoins every step by which it is traversed, a reiterated ambivalence at the heart of agency. Power rearticulated is "re"-articulated in the sense of already done and "re"-articulated in the sense of done over, done again, done anew. What remain to be considered are: (a) how the formation of the subject involves the regulatory formation of the psyche, including how we might rejoin the discourse of power with the discourse of psychoanalysis; and (b) how we might make such a conception of the subject work as a notion of political agency in postliberatory times.

Regulations of the Psyche

If power works not merely to dominate or oppress existing subjects, but also to form subjects, what is this formation? Obviously, power does not bring persons into the world in any ordinary sense. Foucault links the formative or productive character of power to regulatory and disciplinary regimes. In *Discipline and Punish*, crime produces a class of criminals, crafted bodily in the gesture and style of imprisonment. But how are we to understand this sense of production and crafting? The formative dimension of power is to be understood in a nonmechanistic and nonbehavioristic fashion. It does not always produce according to a purpose, or rather, its production is such that it often exceeds or alters the purposes for which it produces.[8] Foucault is notoriously taciturn on the topic of the psyche, but an account of subjection, it seems, must be traced in the turns of psychic life. More specifically, it must be traced in the peculiar turning of a subject against itself that takes place in acts of self-reproach, conscience, and melancholia that work in tandem with processes of social regulation. And yet, if we refuse the ontological dualism that posits the separation of the political and the psychic, it seems crucial to offer a critical account of psychic subjection in terms of the regulatory and productive effects of power. If forms of regulatory power are sustained in part through the formation of a subject, and if that formation takes place according to the requirements of power, specifically, as the incorporation of norms, then a theory of subject formation must give an account of this process of incorporation, and the notion of incorporation must be interrogated to ascertain the psychic topography it assumes. How does the subjection of desire require and institute the desire *for* subjection?

In claiming that social norms are internalized, we have not yet explained what incorporation or, more generally, internalization is, what it means for a norm to become internalized or what happens to the norm in the process of internalization. Is the norm first "outside," and does it then enter into a pre-given psychic space, understood as an interior theater of some kind? Or does the internalization of the norm contribute to the production of internality? Does the norm, having become psychic, involve not only the interiorization of the norm, but the interiorization of the psyche?[9] I argue that this process of internalization *fabricates the distinction between interior and exterior life*, offering us a distinction between the psychic and the social that differs significantly from an account of the psychic internalization of norms. Moreover, given that norms are not internalized in mechanical or fully predictable ways, does the norm assume another character as a *psychic* phenomenon? In particular, how are we to account for the desire for the norm and for subjection more generally in terms of a prior desire for social existence, a desire exploited by regulatory power?

Where social categories guarantee a recognizable and endur-
ing social existence, the embrace of such categories, even as
they work in the service of subjection, is often preferred to no
social existence at all. How is it, then, that the longing for subjection, based on a longing for social existence, recalling and
exploiting primary dependencies, emerges as an instrument
and effect of the power of subjection?

To underscore the abuses of power as real, not the creation
or fantasy of the subject, power is often cast as unequivocally
external to the subject, something imposed against the subject's will. But if the very production of the subject and the
formation of that will are the consequences of a primary subordination, then the vulnerability of the subject to a power not
of its own making is unavoidable. That vulnerability qualifies
the subject as an exploitable kind of being. If one is to oppose
the abuses of power (which is not the same as opposing power
itself), it seems wise to consider in what our vulnerability to
that abuse consists. That subjects are constituted in primary
vulnerability does not exonerate the abuses they suffer; on the
contrary, it makes all the more clear how fundamental the vulnerability can be.

How is it that the subject is the kind of being who can be
exploited, who is, by virtue of its own formation, vulnerable
to subjugation? Bound to seek recognition of its own existence
in categories, terms, and names that are not of its own making,
the subject seeks the sign of its own existence outside itself,
in a discourse that is at once dominant and indifferent. Social
categories signify subordination and existence at once. In other
words, within subjection the price of existence is subordination. Precisely at the moment in which choice is impossible,
the subject pursues subordination as the promise of existence.
This pursuit is not choice, but neither is it necessity. Subjec-

tion exploits the desire for existence, where existence is always conferred from elsewhere; it marks a primary vulnerability to the Other in order to be.

Assuming terms of power that one never made but to which one is vulnerable, on which one depends in order to be, appears to be a mundane subjection at the basis of subject formation. "Assuming" power is no simple process, however, for power is not mechanically reproduced when it is assumed. Instead, on being assumed, power runs the risk of assuming another form and direction. If conditions of power do not unilaterally produce subjects, then what is the temporal and logical form that the assumption of power takes? A redescription of the domain of psychic subjection is needed to make clear how social power produces modes of reflexivity at the same time as it limits forms of sociality. In other words, to the extent that norms operate as psychic phenomena, restricting and producing desire, they also govern the formation of the subject and circumscribe the domain of a livable sociality. The psychic operation of the norm offers a more insidious route for regulatory power than explicit coercion, one whose success allows its tacit operation within the social. And yet, being psychic, the norm does not merely reinstate social power, it becomes formative and vulnerable in highly specific ways. The social categorizations that establish the vulnerability of the subject to language are themselves vulnerable to both psychic and historical change. This view counters an understanding of a psychic or linguistic normativity (as in some versions of the Symbolic) that is prior to the social or sets constraints on the social. Just as the subject is derived from conditions of power that precede it, so the psychic operation of the norm is derived, though not mechanically or predictably, from prior social operations.

Psychic subjection marks a specific modality of subjection.

It does not simply reflect or represent broader relations of social power—even as it remains importantly tied to them. Freud and Nietzsche offer differing accounts of subject formation that rely on the productivity of the norm. Both account for the fabrication of conscience as the effect of an internalized prohibition (thereby establishing "prohibition" as not only privative, but productive). In Freud and Nietzsche, a prohibition on action or expression is said to turn "the drive"[10] back on itself, fabricating an internal sphere, the condition for self-inspection and reflexivity. The drive turning back upon itself becomes the precipitating condition of subject formation, a primary longing in recoil that is traced in Hegel's view of the unhappy consciousness as well. Whether the doubling back upon itself is performed by primary longings, desire, or drives, it produces in each instance a psychic habit of self-beratement, one that is consolidated over time as conscience.

Conscience is the means by which a subject becomes an object for itself, reflecting on itself, establishing itself as reflective and reflexive. The "I" is not simply one who thinks about him- or herself; it is defined by this capacity for reflective self-relation or reflexivity. For Nietzsche, reflexivity is a consequence of conscience; self-knowing follows from self-punishment. (Thus one never "knows" oneself prior to the recoil of desire in question.) In order to curb desire, one makes of oneself an object for reflection; in the course of producing one's own alterity, one becomes established as a reflexive being, one who can take oneself as an object. Reflexivity becomes the means by which desire is regularly transmuted into the circuit of self-reflection. The doubling back of desire that culminates in reflexivity produces, however, another order of desire: the desire for that very circuit, for reflexivity and, ultimately, for subjection.

What is the means by which desire is understood to be curbed, doubled back, or even prohibited? Reflection on desire absorbs desire into reflection: we will see how this works in Hegel. But there is another order of prohibition, one which falls outside the circuit of self-reflection. Freud distinguishes between repression and foreclosure, suggesting that a repressed desire might once have lived apart from its prohibition, but that foreclosed desire is rigorously barred, constituting the subject through a certain kind of preemptive loss. Elsewhere I have suggested that the foreclosure of homosexuality appears to be foundational to a certain heterosexual version of the subject.[11] The formula "I have never loved" someone of similar gender and "I have never lost" any such person predicates the "I" on the "never-never" of that love and loss. Indeed, the ontological accomplishment of heterosexual "being" is traced to this double negation, which forms its constitutive melancholia, an emphatic and irreversible loss that forms the tenuous basis of that "being."

Significantly, Freud identifies heightened conscience and self-beratement as one sign of melancholia, the condition of uncompleted grief. The foreclosure of certain forms of love suggests that the melancholia that grounds the subject (and hence always threatens to unsettle and disrupt that ground) signals an incomplete and irresolvable grief. Unowned and incomplete, melancholia is the limit to the subject's sense of *pouvoir*, its sense of what it can accomplish and, in that sense, its power. Melancholia rifts the subject, marking a limit to what it can accommodate. Because the subject does not, cannot, *reflect* on that loss, that loss marks the limit of reflexivity, that which exceeds (and conditions) its circuitry. Understood as foreclosure, that loss inaugurates the subject and threatens it with dissolution.

Considered along Nietzschean and Hegelian lines, the subject engages in its own self-thwarting, accomplishes its own subjection, desires and crafts its own shackles, and so turns against a desire that it knows to be—or knew to be—its own. For a loss to predate the subject, to make it possible (and impossible), we must consider the part that loss plays in subject formation. Is there a loss that cannot be thought, cannot be owned or grieved, which forms the condition of possibility for the subject? Is this what Hegel called "the loss of the loss," a foreclosure that constitutes an unknowability without which the subject cannot endure, an ignorance and melancholia that makes possible all claims of knowledge as one's own? Is there not a longing to grieve—and, equivalently, an inability to grieve—that which one never was able to love, a love that falls short of the "conditions of existence"? This is a loss not merely of the object or some set of objects, but of love's own possibility: the loss of the ability to love, the unfinishable grieving for that which founds the subject. On the one hand, melancholia is an attachment that substitutes for an attachment that is broken, gone, or impossible; on the other hand, melancholia continues the tradition of impossibility, as it were, that belongs to the attachment for which it substitutes.

There are, of course, various ways of refusing to love, not all of which qualify as foreclosure. But what happens when a certain foreclosure of love becomes the condition of possibility for social existence? Does this not produce a sociality afflicted by melancholia, a sociality in which loss cannot be grieved because it cannot be recognized as loss, because what is lost never had any entitlement to existence?

Here one might well distinguish between (a) an attachment that is subsequently disavowed and (b) a foreclosure that structures the forms that any attachment may assume. In the latter case, the foreclosure might be usefully relinked with the Foucauldian notion of a regulatory ideal, an ideal according to which certain forms of love become possible and others, impossible. Within psychoanalysis, we think of social sanction as encoded in the ego-ideal and patrolled by the super-ego. But what might it mean to think of social sanction as working, through foreclosure, to produce the possible domain in which love and loss can operate? As foreclosure, the sanction works not to prohibit existing desire but to produce certain kinds of objects and to bar others from the field of social production. In this way, the sanction does not work according to the repressive hypothesis, as postulated and criticized by Foucault, but as a mechanism of production, one that can operate, however, on the basis of an originary violence.[12]

In the work of Melanie Klein, guilt appears to emerge, not in consequence of internalizing an external prohibition, but as a way of preserving the object of love from one's own potentially obliterating violence. Guilt serves the function of preserving the object of love and, hence, of preserving love itself. What might it mean to understand guilt, then, as a way in which love preserves the object it might otherwise destroy? As a stopgap against a sadistic destruction, guilt signals less the psychic presence of an originally social and external norm than a countervailing desire to continue the object one wishes dead. It is in this sense that guilt emerges in the course of melancholia not only, as the Freudian view would have it, to keep the dead object alive, but to keep the living object from "death," where death means the death of love, including the occasions of separation and loss.

Does the Kleinian view suggest, then, that the function of love can be fully explained within a psychic economy that carries no socially significant residue? Or is the social signifi-

cance of guilt to be traced in a register other than that of prohibition, in the desire for reparation? In order to preserve the
object from one's own aggression, an aggression that always
accompanies love (as conflict), guilt enters the psychic scene
as a necessity. If the object goes, so goes a source of love. In
one sense, guilt works to thwart the aggressive expression of
love that might do in the loved object, an object understood to
be a source of love; in a counter sense, however, guilt works
to preserve the object as an object of love (its idealization) and
hence (via idealization) to preserve the possibility of loving
and being loved. Aggression—or hate—is not merely miti-
gated, but rerouted against the one who loves, operating as
the self-beratements of the super-ego.[13] Because love and aggression work together, the mitigation of aggression through
guilt is also the mitigation of love. Guilt works, then, both to
foreclose and to continue love, or rather, to continue love (less
passionately, to be sure) as the effect of a foreclosure.

Klein's scheme raises a number of questions relating to the
relation between love and aggression. Why might one want
dead the object of love? Is this a primary sadism that might be
explained by recourse to a primary death drive, or are there
other ways to account for the desire to vanquish what one
loves? Following Freud, Klein situates such a desire to vanquish within the problematic of melancholia, thus making the
point that the desire to vanquish characterizes a relation to an
object already lost: already lost and thus eligible for a certain
kind of vanquishing.

Klein links guilt toward the object with the desire to triumph over the object, a sense of triumph which, if pursued too
far, threatens to destroy the object as a source of love. Yet one
might consider that certain forms of love entail the loss of the
object not only because of an innate desire to triumph, but be-

cause such objects fail to qualify as objects of love: as objects of love they assume a mark of destruction. Indeed, they may threaten one's own destruction as well: "I will be destroyed if I love in that way." Marked for "death," the object is, as it were, already lost, and the desire to vanquish the object is precisely the desire to vanquish an object which, if loved, would spell destruction for the one who loves.

Can we read the workings of social power precisely in the delimitation of the field of such objects, objects marked for death? And is this part of the irreality, the melancholic aggression and the desire to vanquish, that characterizes the public response to the death of many of those considered "socially dead," who die from AIDS? Gay people, prostitutes, drug users, among others? If they are dying or already dead, let us vanquish them again. And can the sense of "triumph" be won precisely through a practice of social differentiation in which one achieves and maintains "social existence" only by the production and maintenance of those socially dead? Might one not also read the paranoia that structures public discourse on such issues as the inversion of that aggression: the desire to vanquish the dead other that, through a reversal, comes to mark that other as the threat of death, casting the other as the (unlikely) persecutor of the socially normal and normalized?

What is it, then, that is desired in subjection? Is it a simple love of the shackles, or is there a more complex scenario at work? How is survival to be maintained if the terms by which existence is guaranteed are precisely those that demand and institute subordination? On this understanding, subjection is the paradoxical effect of a regime of power in which the very "conditions of existence," the possibility of continuing as a recognizable social being, requires the formation and maintenance of the subject in subordination. If one accepts Spinoza's notion that desire is always the desire to persist in one's own being,[14] and recasts the *metaphysical* substance that forms the ideal for desire as a more pliable notion of social being, one might then be prepared to redescribe the desire to persist in one's own being as something that can be brokered only within the risky terms of social life. The risk of death is thus co-extensive with the insurmountability of the social. If the terms by which "existence" is formulated, sustained, and withdrawn are the active and productive vocabulary of power, then to persist in one's being means to be given over from the start to social terms that are never fully one's own. The desire to persist in one's own being requires submitting to a world of others that is fundamentally not one's own (a submission that does not take place at a later date, but which frames and makes possible the desire to be). Only by persisting in alterity does one persist in one's "own" being. Vulnerable to terms that one never made, one persists always, to some degree, through categories, names, terms, and classifications that mark a primary and inaugurative alienation in sociality. If such terms institute a primary subordination or, indeed, a primary violence, then a subject emerges against itself in order, paradoxically, to be for itself.

What would it mean for the subject to desire something other than its continued "social existence"? If such an existence cannot be undone without falling into some kind of death, can existence nevertheless be risked, death courted or pursued, in order to expose and open to transformation the hold of social power on the conditions of life's persistence? The subject is compelled to repeat the norms by which it is produced, but that repetition establishes a domain of risk, for if one fails to reinstate the norm "in the right way," one becomes subject to further sanction, one feels the prevailing conditions of exis-

tence threatened. And yet, without a repetition that risks life—
in its current organization—how might we begin to imagine
the contingency of that organization, and performatively re-
configure the contours of the conditions of life?

A critical analysis of subjection involves: (1) an account of
the way regulatory power maintains subjects in subordination
by producing and exploiting the demand for continuity, visi-
bility, and place; (2) recognition that the subject produced as
continuous, visible, and located is nevertheless haunted by an
inassimilable remainder, a melancholia that marks the limits
of subjectivation; (3) an account of the iterability of the subject that shows how agency may well consist in opposing and
transforming the social terms by which it is spawned.

Although such a formulation can hardly be the basis for an
optimistic view of the subject or of a subject-centered politics,
it may stand as a provocation and as a caution against two
forms of theoretical desire: one in which assuming and stat-
ing a "subject-position" is the consummate moment of politics;
and another in which the dismissal of the subject as a philosophical trope underestimates the linguistic requirements for
entering sociality at all. As much as a perspective on the subject requires an evacuation of the first person, a suspension of
the "I" in the interests of an analysis of subject formation, so
a reassumption of that first-person perspective is compelled
by the question of agency. The analysis of subjection is always
double, tracing the conditions of subject formation and tracing the turn against those conditions for the subject—and its
perspective—to emerge.

A critical evaluation of subject formation may well offer a
better comprehension of the double binds to which our eman-
cipatory efforts occasionally lead without, in consequence,
evacuating the political. Is there a way to affirm complicity

as the basis of political agency, yet insist that political agency may do more than reiterate the conditions of subordination? If, as Althusser implies, becoming a subject requires a kind of mastery indistinguishable from submission, are there perhaps political and psychic consequences to be wrought from such a founding ambivalence? The temporal paradox of the subject is such that, of necessity, we must lose the perspective of a subject already formed in order to account for our own becoming. That "becoming" is no simple or continuous affair, but an uneasy practice of repetition and its risks, compelled yet incomplete, wavering on the horizon of social being.

Stubborn Attachment, Bodily Subjection

Rereading Hegel on the Unhappy Consciousness

a freedom still enmeshed in servitude
—Hegel, *The Phenomenology of Spirit*

The transition in *The Phenomenology of Spirit* from the section "Lordship and Bondage" to "The Freedom of Self-Consciousness: Stoicism, Skepticism, and the Unhappy Consciousness"[1] is one of the least interrogated of Hegel's philosophical movements. Perhaps because the chapter on lordship and bondage secured a liberationist narrative for various progressive political visions, most readers have neglected to pay attention to the resolution of freedom into self-enslavement at the end of the chapter. Insofar as recent theory has called into question both the assumption of a progressive history and the status of the subject, the dystopic resolution of "Lordship and Bondage" has perhaps regained a timely significance.

Foucault suggested that the point of modern politics is no

longer to liberate a subject, but rather to interrogate the regulatory mechanisms through which "subjects" are produced and maintained. Although Foucault's vocabulary ought not to be conflated with Hegel's, his concern with the double-edged implications of subjection (*assujetissement:* the simultaneous *forming* and *regulating* of the subject) is in some ways prefigured in Hegel's account of the bondsman's liberation into various forms of ethical self-beratement. In *Discipline and Punish*, Foucault limits the efficacy of prison reform: "the man described for us, whom we are invited to free, is already in himself the effect of a subjection [*assujettissement*] much more profound than himself."[2] The bondsman in Hegel throws off the apparently external "Lord" only to find himself in an ethical world, subjected to various norms and ideals. Or, to put it more precisely, the subject emerges as an unhappy consciousness through the reflexive application of these ethical laws.

The permutations of self-enslavement that Hegel describes appear to take the body as what must be negated, mortified, or subordinated to an ethical demand. The "terror" that seizes the bondsman with his recognition of freedom appears to culminate in the simultaneous fabrication of ethical norms and the beratement of the bodily condition of his own life. In this sense, "The Unhappy Consciousness" establishes a relation between self-enslavement as bodily subjection and the formulation of self-imposed ethical imperatives that prefigures Nietzsche's critique of the same in *On the Genealogy of Morals* and Foucault's appropriation of that critique. In the following citation from Nietzsche's *Genealogy of Morals*, one can discern a temporary convergence between the figures of self-enslavement in Hegel's "Unhappy Consciousness" and the moralized "man" of conscience in Nietzsche: "This *instinct for freedom* forcibly made latent . . . this instinct for freedom pushed back and repressed, incarcerated within and finally able to discharge and vent itself only on itself: that, and that alone, is what the *bad conscience* is in its beginnings." [3]

Underscoring the painful realization that "liberation" from external authorities does not suffice to initiate a subject into freedom, Foucault draws upon Nietzsche and, in particular, upon the self-incarcerating movement that structures modern forms of reflexivity. The limits to liberation are to be understood not merely as self-imposed but, more fundamentally, as the precondition of the subject's very formation. A certain structuring attachment *to* subjection becomes the condition of moral subjectivation. Consider the expanded text of Foucault's remarks on the prisoner's subjection, previously cited, in *Discipline and Punish*: "The man described for us, whom we are invited to free, is already in himself the effect of a subjection [*assujettissement*] much more profound than himself. A 'soul' inhabits him and brings him to existence, which is itself a factor in the mastery that power exercises over the body. The soul is the effect and instrument of a political anatomy; the soul is the prison of the body." [4]

How precisely are we to read this "inhabiting" of the body by the soul? Can a return to Hegel help us to read it? What are the points of convergence and divergence in Hegel, Nietzsche, and Foucault on the structure of subjection? Hegel's account in "The Unhappy Consciousness" prefigures a critical discourse on ethical positions that not only seek to institute the denial or sacrifice of bodily life, but that fall into instructive paradoxes when they do. Hegel shows that if the suppression of the body requires an instrumental movement of and by the body, then the body is inadvertently *preserved* in and by the instrument of its suppression. This formulation prefigures the possibility of a convergence with Nietzschean, Foucaultian, and, as we shall see, Freudian perspectives on self-abasement, which Hegel's text, in the transition to Spirit, forecloses. The reading that follows pursues the path that Hegel introduces only to foreclose. Arresting the text prior to its resolution into Spirit, this inquiry seeks to know whether a suppressed link with a Nietzschean and Freudian account of conscience is embedded in Hegel's chapter.

The first section of this essay offers a reading that accounts for how this paradox of bodily subjection is formulated in the transition from "Lordship and Bondage" to "The Unhappy Consciousness" in *The Phenomenology of Spirit*. In the second section, I consider the restatements of that paradoxical formulation in psychoanalytic and Foucaultian terms. Without presuming a direct line of influence, I suggest both that Hegel's insights in "The Unhappy Consciousness" on the ineluctability of the attachment of and to the body in subjection are reiterated in Foucaultian frameworks, and that the Foucaultian account of subjection, despite its significant moves beyond dialectical logic, remains unwittingly tethered to the Hegelian formulation. Furthermore, Hegel tacitly presumes that subjection is understood as a self-negating *attachment* and, in this way, shares an operative assumption with the Freudian notion of libidinal investment.

Hegel and the Production of Self-Enslavement

In Hegel's *Phenomenology*, bodies are almost never to be found as objects of philosophical reflection, much less as sites of experience, for bodies are, in Hegel, always and only referred to indirectly as the encasement, location, or specificity of consciousness. By the time we arrive at the section on the unhappy consciousness, we, the readers, have already encountered the lord and the bondsman, and we have been given to understand these discrepant figures as differentially positioned with respect to bodily life. The bondsman appears as an instrumental body whose labor provides for the material conditions of the lord's existence, and whose material products reflect both the subordination of the bondsman and the domination of the master. In a sense, the lord postures as a disembodied desire for self-reflection, one who not only requires the subordination of the bondsman in the status of an instrumental body, but who requires in effect that the bondsman *be* the lord's body, but be it in such a way that the lord forgets or disavows his own activity in producing the bondsman, a production which we will call a projection.

This forgetting involves a clever trick. It is an action by which an activity is disavowed, yet, as an action, it rhetorically concedes the very activity that it seeks to negate. To disavow one's body, to render it "Other" and then to establish the "Other" as an effect of autonomy, is to produce one's body in such a way that the activity of its production—and its essential relation to the lord—is denied. This trick or ruse involves a double disavowal and an imperative that the "Other" become complicit with this disavowal. In order not to be the body that the lord presumably is, and in order to have the bondsman posture as if the body that he is belongs to himself—and not be the orchestrated projection of the lord—there must be a certain kind of exchange, a bargain or deal, in which ruses are enacted and transacted. In effect, the imperative to the bondsman consists in the following formulation: you be my body for me, but do not let me know that the body you are is my body. An injunction and contract are here performed in such a way that the moves which guarantee the fulfillment of the injunction and the contract are immediately covered over and forgotten.

At the close of the section on lordship and bondage, the bondsman labors away in a repetitive fashion on objects that belong to the lord. In this sense, both his labor and his products are presumed from the start to be other than his own, expropriated. They are given away prior to any possibility of giving them away, since they are, strictly speaking, never the bondsman's to give. And yet, this "contract" in which the bondsman substitutes himself for the lord becomes consequential; the substitution itself becomes formative of and for the bondsman. As the bondsman slaves away and becomes aware of his own signature on the things that he makes, he recognizes in the form of the artifact that he crafts the markings of his own labor, markings that are formative of the object itself. His labor produces a visible and legible set of marks in which the bondsman reads back from the object a confirmation of his own formative activity. This labor, this activity, which belongs from the start to the lord, is nevertheless reflected back to the bondsman as his own labor, a labor that emanates from him, even if it appears to emanate from the lord.

Can, then, the labor reflected back be said finally to be the bondsman's own? Remember that the lord has disavowed his own laboring being, his body as an instrument of labor, and has established the bondsman as the one who will occupy the lord's body for him. In this sense, the lord has contracted the bondsman as a surrogate or substitute. The bondsman thus belongs to the lord, but with a kind of belonging that cannot be avowed, for to avow the belonging would be to avow the substitution and, hence, to expose the lord as being the body which the lord apparently very much does not want to be. Hence, it is as a substitute in the service of disavowal that the bondsman labors; only by miming and covering over the mimetic status of that labor can the bondsman appear to be both

active and autonomous. Indeed, the object emerges as the ob-
jectification of the bondsman's labor, and thus as an instance
of that labor, a congealing and reflection of that labor. But
what, then, does the object reflect? Is it the autonomy of the
bondsman? Or is it the dissimulated effect of autonomy that
results from the contract made between lord and bondsman?
In other words, if the bondsman effects autonomy through a
miming of the lord's body, a miming which remains hidden
from the lord, then the "autonomy" of the slave is the credible
effect of this dissimulation. The object of labor thus reflects
the autonomy of the bondsman to the extent that the object,
too, covers over the dissimulation which is the activity of the
bondsman. In his work, then, the bondsman discovers or reads
his own signature, but what is it that marks that signature as
his own? The bondsman discovers his autonomy, but he does
not (yet) see that his autonomy is the dissimulated effect of
the lord's. (Nor does he see that the lord's autonomy is itself
a dissimulation: the lord effects the autonomy of disembodied
reflection and delegates the autonomy of embodiment to the
bondsman, thus producing two "autonomies" that appear at
the outset radically to exclude one another.)

But here a question emerges: Does the bondsman's activity
remain fully constrained by the dissimulation by which it is
mobilized? Or does this dissimulation produce effects that exceed the control or dominion of the lord?

If the bondsman is to recognize the marks made on the
object as his own, then that recognition must take place
through an act of reading or interpretation by which the marks
(*Zeichen*) that the bondsman sees are somehow understood to
represent the bondsman. It is not that the activity must be witnessed, but that the *signs* produced must be read as an effect
of the effectivity that designates the bondsman, must in some

way be understood to refer retroactively to the bondsman as signatory. If we are to understand the forming of the object as the inscribing of the bondsman's signature, the formative principle of the object *to be* the formation of his signature, then the bondsman's signature designates a domain of contested ownership. This is *his* mark, which he can read (we shall let the bondsman occupy the site of presumptive masculinity), and so the object appears to belong to him. Yet this object marked by him, which has his mark on it, belongs to the lord, at least nominally. The bondsman signs, as it were, for the lord, as a proxy signatory, as a delegated substitute. Thus the signature does not seal ownership of the object by the bondsman, but becomes the site for the redoubling of ownership and, hence, sets the stage for a scene of contestation.

The mark or sign on the object is not simply the property of the bondsman—this object with his mark on it implies for him that he is a being who marks things, whose activity produces a singular effect, a signature, which is irreducibly his. That signature is erased when the object is given over to the lord, who stamps it with *his* name, owns it, or consumes it in some way. The working of the slave is thus to be understood as a marking which regularly unmarks itself, a signatory act which puts itself under erasure at the moment in which it is circulated, for circulation here is always a matter of expropriation by the lord. The slave, of course, from the start has been working for another, under the name or sign of some other, and so has been marking the object with his own signature under a set of conditions in which that signature is always already erased, written over, expropriated, resignified. If the bondsman writes over the signatory of the lord, temporarily reversing the subordinate position of the proxy to the original, the lord reappropriates the object by writing over the signature of the bondsman. What emerges is less a palimpsestic object—like Kafka's topographies—than a mark of ownership produced through a set of consequential erasures.

Significantly, the bondsman nevertheless derives a sense of self-recognition at the end of the chapter, but not by reading back his signature from the object. After all, that signature has been written over by the signature of the lord. He recognizes himself in the very forfeiture of the signature, in the *threat to* autonomy that such an expropriation produces. Strangely, then, a certain self-recognition is derived from the radically tenuous status of the bondsman; it is achieved through the experience of *absolute fear*.

This fear is a fear *of* a certain loss of control, a certain transience and expropriability produced by the activity of labor. Here the logic of the bondsman's activity appears curiously to converge with that of the lord. Earlier it seemed that the lord occupied the place of pure consumption, appropriating and extinguishing all that the bondsman made. The bondsman, by contrast, achieved the experience of self-reflexivity through working on and creating an object that bore the marks of his being, and thereby understood himself as a being who forms or creates things which outlast him, a producer of permanent things. For the lord, occupying the position of pure consumption, objects were transitory, and he himself was defined as a series of transitory desires. For the lord, then, nothing seemed to last, except perhaps his own consuming activity, his own endless desire.

These two positions, however, are not radically opposed to one another, for each in a different way experiences only and always the loss of the object and, with that loss, the experience of a fearful transience. Work is, for Hegel, a form of desire, a form which ideally suppresses the transitory character of desire; in his words, "work is desire held in check, fleetingness staved off" (118/153). To work on an object is to give it form, and to give it form is to give it an existence that overcomes transitoriness. The consumption of the object is the negation of that effect of permanence; the consumption of the object is its *de*formation. The accumulation of property, however, requires that formed objects be possessed rather than consumed; only as property do objects retain their form and "stave off fleetingness." Only as property do objects fulfill the theological promise with which they are invested.

The bondsman's fear, then, consists in the experience of having what appears to be his property expropriated. In the experience of giving up what he has made, the bondsman understands two issues: first, that what he is is embodied or signified in what he makes, and second, that what he makes is made under the compulsion to give it up. Hence, if the object defines him, reflects back what he is, is the signatory text by which he acquires a sense of who he is, and if those objects are relentlessly sacrificed, then he is a relentlessly self-sacrificing being. He can recognize his own signature only as what is constantly being erased, as a persistent site of vanishing. He has no control over what he puts his name to or over the purposes to which he seeks to fasten his name. His signature is an act of self-erasure: he reads that the signature is his, that his own existence appears to be irreducibly his own, that what is irreducibly his own is his own vanishing, and that this vanishing is effected by another—that is, that this is a socially compelled form of self-erasure. Not only does he labor for another, who takes the yield of his labor, but he gives up his signature for the signature of the other, no longer marking ownership of his own labor in any way.

This expropriation of the object does not negate the bondsman's sense of himself as a laboring being, but it does imply that whatever he makes, he also loses. The determinate thing that the bondsman makes reflects the bondsman himself as a determinate thing. But because the object is given away, he becomes that which can be forfeited. If the object is the congealing or forming of labor, and if the labor is that of the bondsman, then the determinate and transient character of the thing will imply the determinate and transient character of the bondsman. The laboring body which now knows itself to have formed the object also knows that it is *transient*. The bondsman not only negates things (in the sense of transforming them through labor) and is a negating activity, but he is subject to a full and final negation in death. This confrontation of death at the end of the chapter recalls the life-and-death struggle at its beginning. The strategy of domination was meant to replace the life-and-death struggle. But in the earlier version death happened through the violence of the other; domination was a way of forcing the other to die *within* the context of life. The failure of domination as a strategy reintroduces the fear of death, but locates it as the inevitable fate of any being whose consciousness is determined and embodied, no longer as a threat posed by another. The bondsman verges on this shattering recognition of his own death in the last paragraph of the chapter, but he recoils from recognizing death, attaching himself instead to various attributes of his own, taking up a posture of smugness or stubbornness, clinging to what appears to be firm about himself, firmly clinging to himself, in order not to know that death threatens every aspect of his own firmness: "since the entire contents of its natural consciousness have not been jeopardized, [*Indem nicht alle Erfüllungen seines naturlichen*

Bewusstseins wankend geworden] determinate being still *in principle* attaches to it; having a mind of one's own is self-will, a freedom still enmeshed in servitude" (119/155).

The unhappy consciousness emerges here in the movement by which terror is allayed through a resolution of stubbornness or, rather, through the action by which terror of bodily death is displaced by a smugness and stubbornness that, in the next chapter, is revalued as religious self-righteousness. This sanctimonious self is not *without* terror: its reflexivity is self-terrorizing. The body which the bondsmen emblematized as a laboring instrument is recast at the end of the lordship and bondage chapter as a transient object, subject to death. The recognition of the body's death is averted, however, for a mode of living in which the body is ceaselessly dying away: hence, the move from the servitude of the bondsman to that of the unhappy consciousness. The bondsman takes the place of the lord by recognizing his own formative capacity, but once the lord is displaced, the bondsman becomes lord over himself, more specifically, lord over his own body; this form of reflexivity signals the passage from bondage to unhappy consciousness. It involves splitting the psyche into two parts, a lordship and a bondage internal to a single consciousness, whereby the body is again dissimulated as an alterity, but where this alterity is now interior to the psyche itself. No longer subjected as an external instrument of labor, the body is still split off from consciousness. Reconstituted as an interior alien, the body is sustained through its disavowal as what consciousness must continue to disavow.

What is the form that this self-subjection takes in the section on the unhappy consciousness? In the first instance, it is a form of stubbornness (*eigensinnigkeit*). It has a "mind of one's own" or "self-will," but one which is nevertheless still a form of servitude. Consciousness clings or attaches to itself, and this clinging to consciousness is at the same time a disavowal of the body, which appears to signify the terror of death, "the absolute fear." The unhappy consciousness requires and engages this attachment by invoking an imperative. Its fear is allayed by legislating an ethical norm. Hence, the imperative to cling to oneself is motivated by this absolute fear and by the need to refuse that fear. Inasmuch as it is an *ethical* injunction, this imperative is the disarticulated refusal of absolute fear.

The section on the unhappy consciousness explains the genesis of the sphere of the ethical as a defense against the absolute fear by which it is motivated. The fabrication of norms out of (and against) fear, and the reflexive imposition of those norms, subjects the unhappy consciousness in a double sense: the subject is subordinated to norms, and the norms are subjectivating, that is, they give an ethical shape to the reflexivity of this emerging subject. The subjection that takes place under the sign of the ethical is a flight from fear, and so is constituted as a kind of flight and denial, a fearful flight from fear that covers its fear first with stubborness and then with religious self-righteousness. The more absolute the ethical imperative becomes, the more stubborn or *eigensinnig* the enforcement of its law, the more the absoluteness of the motivating fear is at once articulated and refused. Absolute fear is thus displaced by the absolute law which, paradoxically, reconstituted the fear as a fear *of* the law.

Absolute fear would jeopardize all determinate things, including the determinate thingness of the bondsman. The flight from that fear, a fear of death, vacates the thinglike character of the subject. This entails vacating the body and clinging to what appears to be most disembodied: thought. Hegel introduces stoicism as a kind of defensive clinging, one that separates the activity of thinking from any content. For Hegel, stoicism withdraws into a subjective and rational existence that has as its highest aim the absolute withdrawal from existence per se, including its own. This task turns out to be self-refuting, of course, insofar as even self-refutation requires a persistent self to enact the withdrawal from its own and other existences. Because the conceptual act of negation always presupposes a position from which that negation takes place, stoicism ends up underscoring the very positivity of the self that it sought to deny. Skepticism follows upon stoicism for Hegel because skepticism begins by presupposing the insuperability of the thinking subject. For skepticism, the self is a perpetually negating activity, actively refuting the existence of everything as its own constitutive activity.

Skepticism negates the domain of alterity by trying to show that any given determination of logical necessity turns into its opposite and, hence, is not what it is. The skeptic traces and focuses on this constant vanishing of determinate appearance without taking into account the dialectical logic that orchestrates and unifies these various oppositions. Hence, nothing is what it is, and there is no logical or empirical ground accessible to the skeptic on which the domain of alterity might rationally be known. The skeptic's thinking becomes a frantic effort to make every given determination disappear into some other one, so that this constant appearing and vanishing proceeds according to no order or necessity. The skeptic, like some new historicists among us, ends up producing contradiction for its own sake: significantly, Hegel argues that this production of chaos (understood as ceaseless contradiction) is *pleasurable* inasmuch as the skeptic is always able to undermine the position of his philosophical opponent.

This kind of pleasurable and incessant refutation is still a form of stubbornness or *eigensinnigkeit*: "it is in fact like the squabbling of self-willed children [*eigensinniger Jungen*] who by contradicting themselves buy for themselves the pleasure [*die Freude*] of continually contradicting one another" (126/162). The skeptic overrides his own contradictoriness in order to take pleasure in forcing others to witness their contradictions. But this pleasure, a form of sadism, is short-lived, for the stubborn and persistent character of the skeptic's efforts will doubtless be challenged when the skeptic encounters another like himself. If another skeptic exposes the first skeptic's contradictions, then the first skeptic is forced to take account of his own contradictoriness. This understanding of his own contradictoriness will initiate for him a new modality of thought. At this point, the skeptic becomes self-conscious of the constitutive contradiction of his own negating activity and the unhappy consciousness emerges as an explicit form of ethical reflexivity.

In a sense, the childish and stubborn pleasure that the skeptic takes in watching another fall turns into a profound unhappiness when he is, as it were, forced *to watch himself* fall into endless contradictions. Here the distance afforded by watching seems essentially linked to the sadism of the pleasure and to the posture of the skeptic as one who exempts himself through visual distance from the scene that he witnesses. The sadistic pleasure involved in watching another becomes, in the mode of unhappiness, a displeasurable watching of oneself.[5] Witnessing implies a mimetic reduplication of the self, and its "dispassion" is belied by the passion of mimeticism. The self who shored up its identity by encouraging others to fall into contradiction suddenly sees itself as one of those others; this viewing of oneself at a distance not only initiates the unhappy consciousness but also inverts the skeptic's pleasure into pain.

The sadism directed toward the other is now turned back on consciousness itself (postponing for the moment whether the pleasure in sadism is also rerouted against consciousness). As a dual structure, the unhappy consciousness takes itself as its own object of scorn.

The philosophical elaboration of this scorn takes the following form: consciousness is now divided into two parts, the "essential" and "unchangeable," on the one hand, and the "inessential" and "changeable," on the other. The watching self, defined as a kind of *witnessing* and *scorning*, differentiates itself from the self witnessed as perpetually falling into contradiction. This watching becomes a way of *re*establishing the visual distance between a subject aloof from the scene and the subject in contradiction. In this case, however, the witnessing and scorning self cannot deny that the contradictory self is its own self; it knows that the contradictory self is *itself*, but in order to shore up an identity over and against it, it renders this contradictory self into an *in*essential part of itself. It thus parts with itself in order to purify itself of contradiction.

As a result, the unhappy consciousness berates itself constantly, setting up one part of itself as a pure judge aloof from contradiction and disparaging its changeable part as inessential, although ineluctably tied to it. Significantly, the activity that in skepticism begins as childish sadism becomes reformulated as ethical self-judgment in the context of the unhappy consciousness: as adult to child, then, the unchangeable consciousness "passes judgment" on the changeable. Implicit in this dual structuring of the subject, however, is the relation between thought and corporeality, for the unchangeable will be a kind of noncontradictory thought, the pure thought sought by the stoics, and the contradictory domain will be that of alternating qualities, the changeable domain of appearance, what pertains to the subject's own phenomenal being. The child who "watches" is transfigured into the judge who "passes judgment," and the aspect of the self on which it passes judgment is steeped in the changeable world of bodily sensation.

Unhappy consciousness seeks to overcome this duality by finding a body which embodies the purity of its unchangeable part; it seeks to come into relation with "the Unchangeable in its incarnate or embodied form." To do this, the subject subordinates its own body in the service of the thought of the unchangeable; this subordinating and purifying effort is that of *devotion* (*Andacht*). Yet, predictably, this effort to deploy the body in the service of thinking the unchangeable proves impossible. Devotion turns out to be pure self-feeling, what Hegel disparagingly refers to as "the chaotic jingling of bells, or a mist of warm incense, a musical thinking" (131/168). As self-feeling, it is the feeling of the body compelled to signify the transcendent and unchangeable, a feeling which nevertheless remains ensconced in the bodily feeling that it seeks to transcend. Indeed, self-feeling refers only and endlessly to itself (a transcendentalized form of *eigensinnigkeit*), and so is unable to furnish knowledge of anything other than itself. Devotion, then, which seeks to instrumentalize the body in the service of the unchangeable, turns out to be an immersion in the body that precludes access to anything else, indeed, an immersion that takes the body to be the unchangeable and so falls into contradiction.

Although devotion appears to be a form of self-immersion, it is also a continuation of self-beratement as self-mortification. This self-feeling, precisely because it does not reach the unchangeable, becomes itself the object of derision and judgment, marking the continuing inadequacy of the self in relation to its transcendent measure. The transcendent is what is always missed, and so haunts this consciousness as a figure of what is permanently inaccessible, forever lost. In the mode of devotion, then, "consciousness . . . can only find as a present reality the grave of its life" (132/169–70). In a transposition of figures, the body survives, and all that is left of the transcendent ideal is a "grave." Whereas devotion, then, begins as an effort to subordinate the body to a transcendent object, it ends by taking the body, that is, self-feeling, as its object of worship, and letting the unchangeable spirit die.

Here we might conclude that a certain form of self-preoccupation, understood as a reformulation of an insurmountable *eigensinnigkeit*, constitutes a narcissism of the subject that defeats the self-sacrificial project of devotion. The subject who would subordinate its body to an ideal, compel its body to embody an ideal, finds itself more fully autonomous from that ideal, outliving it altogether. The collapse of devotion into narcissism, if we can call it that, signifies that there can be no final leave-taking of the body within life. Forced, then, to accept this ineluctability of the body as a presupposition, a new form of the subject emerges, which is distinctly Kantian. If there is a world of appearance for which the body is essential, then surely there is a world of noumena in which the body has no place; the world divides up into beings that are for-itself and in-itself.

In a formulation that will prefigure Kierkegaard's *Philosophical Fragments*, Hegel claims that the unchangeable world surrenders or renounces an embodied form, that it, the in-itself, delivers an embodied version of itself into the changeable world to be sacrificed. This reference to the figure of Christ suggests that the unchangeable world becomes embodied, but does so only to be sacrificed or returned to the unchangeable world from which it came. As a model for the sacred life, Christ is understood as an embodiment which is continually in the mode of giving thanks. In its desire and in its work, this embodied consciousness seeks to give thanks for its own life, capacities, faculties, abilities. These are given to it; its life is experienced as a gift; and it lives out its life in the mode of gratefulness. All of its acts it owes to another; its life becomes understood as a kind of endless debt.

Precisely because, on the one hand, this living being owes its life to another being, it is not the seat or origin of its own actions. Its action is referred to another's action; thus, not being the ground of its own action, it is not responsible for what it does. On the other hand, its own actions are to be construed as a perpetual self-sacrifice by which the self *proves* or demonstrates its own thankfulness. This demonstration of thankfulness thus becomes a kind of self-aggrandizement, what Hegel will call "the extreme of individuality" (134/171).

The renunciation of the self as the origin of its own actions must be performed repeatedly and can never finally be achieved, if only because the *demonstration* of renunciation is itself a self-willed action. This self-willed action thus rhetorically confounds precisely what it is supposed to show. The self becomes an incessant performer of renunciation, whereby the performance, as an action, contradicts the postulation of *in*action that it is meant to signify. Paradoxically, performance becomes the *occasion* for a grand and endless action that effectively augments and individuates the self it seeks to deny.

This consciousness, like the stoic, seeks to know and show itself as a "nothing," yet inevitably becomes a *doing* of nothing. Here the pleasure which earlier appeared to belong to the childish sadism of the skeptic is turned on the self: this "doing of nothing," Hegel argues, finds in "its enjoyment a feeling of wretchedness." This intermingling of pleasure and pain results from a renunciation of the self which can never quite accomplish that renunciation, which, as an incessant accomplishing, carries with it the pleasurable assertion of self. The self-absorption of consciousness does not translate into self-congratulation or simple narcissism. Rather, it appears as negative narcissism, an engaged preoccupation with what is most debased and defiled about it.

Here again the self to be renounced is figured as a bodily self, as "this actual individual in the animal functions." Hegel appears to imply defecation as an object of self-preoccupation: "these [animal functions] are no longer performed naturally and without embarrassment, as matters trifling in themselves which cannot possess any importance or essential significance for Spirit; instead, it is in them that the enemy reveals himself in his characteristic shape, they are rather the object of serious endeavor, and become precisely matters of the utmost importance. This enemy, however, renews himself in his defeat, and consciousness, in fixing its attention on him, far from freeing itself from him, really remains forever in contact with him, and forever sees itself as defiled" (135–36/174). This "enemy," as it were, is described as "the merest particular of the meanest character," one which serves, unfortunately, as an object of identification for this "fallen" consciousness. Here, consciousness in its full abjection has become like shit, lost in a self-referential anality, a circle of its own making. In Hegel's words, "we have here only a personality confined to its own self and its petty actions, a personality brooding over itself, as wretched as it is impoverished" (136/174).

Regarding itself as a nothing, as a doing of nothing, as an excremental function, and hence regarding itself as excrement, this consciousness effectively reduces itself to the changeable features of its bodily functions and products. Yet, since it is an experience *of* wretchedness, there is some consciousness which takes stock of these functions and which is not thoroughly identified with them. Significantly, it is here, in the effort to differentiate itself from its excretory functions, indeed, from its excretory identity, that consciousness relies on a "mediator," what Hegel will call "the priest." In order to reconnect with the pure and the unchangeable, this bodily consciousness offers up its every "doing" to a priest or minister. This mediating agency relieves the abject consciousness of its responsibility for its own actions. Through the institution of counsel and advice, the priest offers the reason for the abject consciousness's actions. Everything that the abject consciousness offers, that is, all of its externalizations, including desire, work, and excrement, are to be construed as *offerings*, as paying penance. The priest institutes bodily self-abnegation as the price of holiness, elevating the renunciatory gesture of excretion to a religious practice whereby the entire body is ritualistically purged. The sanctification of abjection takes place through rituals of fasting and mortification [*fasten und kasteien*]" (137/175). Because the body cannot be fully denied, as the stoic thought, it must be ritualistically renounced.

In its fastings and mortifications, the unhappy consciousness denies itself the pleasures of consumption, figuring perhaps that it will forestall the inevitability of the excremental moment. As self-inflicted bodily acts, fasting and mortification are reflexive actions, turnings of the body against itself. At the limits of this self-mortification and self-sacrifice, the abjected consciousness appears to ground its action in the counsel of the priest, and yet this grounding merely conceals the reflexive origins of its self-punishment.

At this juncture Hegel departs from what has been the pattern of explanation, in which a *self-negating* posture is under-

scored as a *posture*, a phenomenalization that refutes the negation it seeks to institute. In the place of such an explanation,
Hegel asserts that the will of another operates through the self-
sacrificial actions of the penitent. In effect, self-sacrifice is not
refuted through the claim that self-sacrifice is itself a willful
activity; rather, Hegel asserts that in self-sacrifice one enacts
another's will. One might expect that the penitent would be
shown to be reveling in himself, self-aggrandizing, narcissistic, that his self-punishments would culminate in a pleasurable
assertion of self. But Hegel eschews this explanation and thus
breaks with the pattern of explanation in the chapter in favor
of a religious solution in Spirit.

Indeed, at this juncture one might well imagine a set of
closing transitions for "The Unhappy Consciousness" different from the ones Hegel supplies, a set that is, nevertheless,
perhaps more properly Hegelian than Hegel himself. The penitent disclaims his act as his own, avowing that another's will,
the priest's, operates through his self-sacrifice, and, further,
that the priest's will is determined by God's. Installed thus
in a great chain of wills, the abject consciousness enters into
a community of wills. Although its will is determinate, it is
nevertheless bound to the priest's; in this unity, the notion of
Spirit is first discerned. The mediator or priest counsels the
penitent that his pain will be repaid with everlasting abundance, that his misery will be rewarded with everlasting happiness; misery and pain imply a future transformation into
their opposites. In this sense, the minister reformulates the
dialectical reversal and establishes the inversion of values as
an absolute principle. Whereas in all of the earlier examples
of self-negation pleasure was understood to *inhere* in pain
(the pleasurable aggrandizement of the stoic, the pleasurable
sadism of the skeptic), pleasure is here temporally removed

from pain, figured as its future compensation. For Hegel, this eschatological transformation of the pain of this world into the pleasure of the next establishes the transition from self-consciousness to reason. And self-consciousness's recognition of itself as part of a religious community of wills effects the transition from self-consciousness to Spirit.

But what are we to make of this final transition, considering the immanent relation of pleasure and pain in the transitions that precede it? Before the introduction of the "mediator" and the "priest," the chapter on the unhappy consciousness appears to proceed as if it contained a trenchant critique of ethical imperatives and religious ideals, a critique which prefigures the Nietzschean analysis that emerges some sixty years later. Every effort to reduce itself to inaction or to nothing, to subordinate or mortify its own body, culminates inadvertently in the *production* of self-consciousness as a pleasure-seeking and self-aggrandizing agent. Every effort to overcome the body, pleasure, and agency proves to be nothing other than the assertion of precisely those features of the subject.

Post-Hegelian Subjections

The Nietzschean critique of ethical norms, prefigured in "The Unhappy Consciousness" and articulated in Nietzsche's *On the Genealogy of Morals* and *Daybreak*, has received more recent reformulation in Foucault's *Discipline and Punish*. Both Hegel's position and those inspired by Nietzsche might also be usefully compared with Freud's critique of the genesis of moral imperatives in *Civilization and Its Discontents*. Recall that for Hegel ethical imperatives first emerge in a defensive response to absolute fear, and their emergence must be construed as a permutation and refusal of that fear. This absolute fear was the fear of death, hence a fear conditioned by the finite character of the body. The ethical refusal and subordination of the body might then be understood as a magical effort to preempt that existential negation. Moreover, the ideal of radical self-sufficiency is jeopardized by the body's permeability and dependency. In this sense, excretion is not the only "animal function" that would signify "defilement" for this subject. The repeated efforts to sacrifice the body which become repeated assertions of the body are also efforts to defend it against everything that "jeopardizes" it, where to be in "jeopardy" denotes a danger slightly less dire than death, a kind of penetrative paroxysm that implies being moved or shaken sexually "through and through" (*durch und durch angesteckt*). One could then see in the various forms of self-beratement and self-mortification typologized in "The Unhappy Consciousness" a prefiguration of neurosis and perhaps also a specific modality of homosexual panic.[6]

We might then reread the mobilizing fear that is both refused and rerouted by the ethical imperative in terms of the feared "expropriability" of the body. If the bondsman's laboring activity could be expropriated by the lord and the essence of the bondsman's body be held in ownership by that lord, then the body constitutes a site of contested ownership, one which through domination or the threat of death can always be owned by another. The body appears to be nothing other than a threat to the project of safety and self-sufficiency that governs the *Phenomenology*'s trajectory. The anal preoccupation that directly precedes the ascendance into a religious concept of an afterlife suggests that bodily permeability can only be resolved by escape into an afterlife in which no bodies exist at all. This affirmation of the absolute negation of the body contradicts all the earlier efforts to subordinate or master the body *within* life, efforts which culminated in the assertion of the ineluctability of the body. Whereas other religious notions turned out to be surreptitious ways of reasserting the body, this one appears exempt from the dialectical reversal that it resolves.

Psychoanalysis theorizes the failure to maintain the subjection of the body along lines parallel to these earlier dialectical reversals. The repression of the libido is always understood as itself a libidinally invested repression. Hence, the libido is not absolutely negated through repression, but rather becomes the instrument of its own subjection. The repressive law is not external to the libido that it represses, but the repressive law represses to the extent that repression becomes a libidinal activity.[7] Further, moral interdictions, especially those that are turned against the body, are themselves sustained by the bodily activity that they seek to curb:

An idea . . . which belongs entirely to psychoanalysis and which is foreign to people's ordinary way of thinking . . . it tells us that conscience (or more correctly, the anxiety which later becomes conscience) is indeed the cause of instinctual renunciation to begin with, but that later that relationship is reversed. Every renunciation of instinct now becomes a dynamic source of conscience and every fresh renunciation increases the latter's severity and intolerance.[8]

According to Freud, then, the self-imposed imperatives of conscience are pursued and applied precisely because they are now the site of the very satisfaction that they seek to prohibit. In other words, prohibition becomes the displaced site of satisfaction for the "instinct" or desire that is prohibited, an occasion for reliving the instinct under the rubric of the condemning law. This is, of course, the source of the form of comedy in which the bearer of the moral law turns out to be the most serious transgressor of its precepts (Hawthorne's Dimsdale, Tom Stoppard's moral philosopher). Because this displaced satisfaction is experienced through the application of the law, that application is reinvigorated and intensified with the emergence of every prohibited desire. The prohibition does not seek to obliterate prohibited desire; on the contrary, prohibition seeks to reproduce prohibited desire and becomes intensified through the renunciations it effects. The "afterlife" of prohibited desire is in the prohibition itself, where the prohibition not only sustains, but is *sustained by*, the desire that it forces the subject to renounce. In this sense, then, renunciation takes place *through* the very desire that is renounced, which is to say, the desire is *never* renounced, but becomes preserved and reasserted in the very structure of renunciation.

Nietzsche makes a similar argument, deploying a dialectical structure not unlike Hegel's, in his critique of the ascetic ideal in *On the Genealogy of Morals*. The ineluctability of the body in "The Unhappy Consciousness" parallels the ineluctability of "instinct" in Freud and that of the will in Nietzsche. For Nietzsche, the ascetic ideal, understood as a will to nothingness, is a way of interpreting all suffering as guilt. Although guilt works to deny a specific kind of object for human wants, it cannot obliterate the wanting character of humans. According to the dictates of guilt, then, "man had only to *want* something—and to begin with, it mattered not what, whereto, or how he wanted: *the will itself was saved.*" The ascetic ideal, very much like Hegel's unhappy consciousness, is to be understood, then, as:

that hatred against everything human, even more, against everything animal, everything material, this disgust with the senses, with reason itself, this fear of happiness and beauty, this desire to get away from all semblance, change, becoming, death, wish, desire itself—the meaning of all this is a will to nothingness, a will running counter to life, a revolt against the most fundamental presuppositions of life; yet it is and remains a will! . . . rather than want nothing, man even wants nothingness![9]

I do not mean to suggest that Freud's highly problematic notion of instinct, Hegel's inchoate body, and Nietzsche's will are strictly equivalent. Yet I do want to suggest that these three thinkers circumscribe a kind of dialectical reversal which centers on the impossibility of a full or final reflexive suppression of what we might loosely call "the body" within the confines of life. If the suppression of the body is itself an instrumental movement of and by the body, then the body is inadvertently preserved in and by the instrument of its suppression. The self-defeating effort of such suppression, however, not only leads to its opposite—a self-congratulatory or self-aggrandizing assertion of desire, will, the body—in more contemporary formulations it leads to the elaboration of an institution of the subject which exceeds the dialectical frame by which it is spawned.

In Hegel, the suppression of bodily life is shown to require the very body that it seeks to suppress; in this sense, the body is preserved in and by the very act of suppression. Freud understood this differently in his analysis of neurosis as a kind of libidinal attachment to a prohibition which nevertheless thwarts libidinal gratification. Where that thwarting constitutes a repression, the splitting off of ideation from affect, neurosis or symptom formation follows. One might read Hegel's references to *eigensinnigkeit* or stubbornness as illustrating the process of splitting and defense in the formation of neurosis. That Hegel refers to this "unhappiness" as a kind of stubborn attachment suggests that, as in neurosis, the ethical regulation of bodily impulse becomes the focus and aim of impulse itself. In both cases, we are given to understand an attachment to subjection which is formative of the reflexive structure of subjection itself. The impulse or bodily experience which would be negated, to return to Hegel, is inadvertently *preserved* by the very activity of negation.

We can see in both Hegel and Freud a certain reliance on a dialectical reversal by which a bodily experience, broadly construed, comes under the censor of the law only to reemerge as the sustaining affect of that law. The Freudian notion of *sublimation* suggests that denial or displacement of pleasure and desire can become formative of culture; his *Civilization and Its Discontents* thus laid the ground for Marcuse's *Eros and Civilization*. The inadvertently productive effects of sublimation in the formation of cultural products appear to exceed the dialectical reversal by which they are generated. Whereas for Marcuse, the drives, or eros and thanatos, precede the regulatory imperatives by which they are rendered culturally livable, for Foucault, the repressive hypothesis, which appears to include within its structure the model of sublimation, fails to work precisely because repression generates the very pleasures and desires it seeks to regulate. For Foucault, repression does not act on a pregiven field of pleasure and desire; it constitutes that field as that which is to be regulated, that which is always potentially or actually under the rubric of regulation. The repressive regime, as Foucault calls it, requires its own self-augmentation and proliferation. As such, this regime requires the field of bodily impulse to expand and proliferate as a moralized domain, such that it will continually have fresh material through which to articulate its own power. Hence, repression produces a field of infinitely moralizable bodily phenomena in order to facilitate and rationalize its own proliferation.

Here we see that Foucault departs from the kind of dialectical reversal we followed in Hegel. In Foucault, the suppression of the body not only requires and produces the very body it seeks to suppress, it goes further by extending the bodily domain to be regulated, proliferating sites of control, discipline, and suppression. In other words, the body *presumed* by the Hegelian explanation is incessantly produced and proliferated in order to extend the domain of juridical power. In this sense, the restrictions placed *on* the body not only *require* and *produce* the body they seek to restrict, but *proliferate* the domain of the bodily beyond the domain targeted by the original restriction. In what many have come to see as a finally utopian gesture in Foucault, this proliferation of the body by juridical regimes beyond the terms of dialectical reversal is also the site of possible resistance. The psychoanalytic discourse that would describe and pathologize repressed desire ends up producing a discursive incitement to desire: impulse is continually fabricated as a site of confession and, hence, potential control, but this fabrication exceeds the regulatory aims by which it is generated. In this sense, criminal codes which seek to catalogue and institutionalize normalcy become the site for a contestation of the concept of the normal; sexologists who would classify and pathologize homosexuality inadvertently provide the conditions for a proliferation and mobilization of homosexual cultures.

Within the Hegelian framework, the subject, which splits itself off from its body, requires that body in order to sustain its splitting activity; the body to be suppressed is thus marshalled in the service of that suppression. For Foucault, the body to be regulated is similarly marshalled in the service of suppression, but the body is not constituted prior to that regulation. On the contrary, the body is produced *as* an object of regulation, and for regulation to augment itself, the body is *proliferated* as an object of regulation. This proliferation both marks off Foucault's theory from Hegel's and constitutes the site of potential resistance to regulation. The possibility of this resistance is derived from what is *unforeseeable* in proliferation. But to understand how a regulatory regime could produce effects which are not only unforeseeable but constitute resistance, it seems that we must return to the question of stubborn attachments and, more precisely, to the place of that attachment in the subversion of the law.

Although Foucault criticizes Freud's hypothesis of repression, he is indebted to this theorization in his own account of the production and proliferation of the regulated body. In particular, the logic of subjection in both Hegel and Freud implies that the instrument of suppression becomes the new structure and aim of desire, at least when subjection proves effective. But if a regulatory regime requires the production of new sites of regulation and, hence, a more thoroughgoing moralization of the body, then what is the place of bodily impulse, desire, and attachment? Does the regulatory regime not only produce desire, but become produced by the cultivation of a certain attachment *to* the rule of subjection? If part of what regulatory regimes do is to constrain the formation and attachments of desire, then it seems that from the start a certain detachability of impulse is presumed, a certain incommensurability between the capacity for a bodily attachment, on the one hand, and the site where it is confined, on the other. Foucault appears to presume precisely this detachability of desire in claiming that incitements and reversals are to some degree *unforeseeable*, that they have the capacity, central to the notion of resistance, to *exceed* the regulatory aims for which they were produced. If a given regime cannot fully control the incitements that it nevertheless produces, is that in part the result

of a resistance, at the level of impulse, to a full and final domestication by any regulatory regime?

What Hegel implies in "The Unhappy Consciousness" is
not merely that moral wretchedness cannot be coherently sustained, that it invariably concedes the bodily being that it
seeks to deny, but that the pursuit of wretchedness, the attachment to wretchedness, is both the condition and the potential undoing of such subjection. If wretchedness, agony, and
pain are sites or modes of stubbornness, ways of attaching to
oneself, negatively articulated modes of reflexivity, then that
is because they are given by regulatory regimes as the sites
available for attachment, and a subject will attach to pain
rather than not attach at all. For Freud, an infant forms a
pleasure-giving attachment to any excitation that comes its
way, even the most traumatic, which accounts for the formation of masochism and, for some, the production of abjection,
rejection, wretchedness, and so on as the necessary precondi-
tions for love. The gesture of rejection can become masoch-
istically eroticized only because it is a gesture. Although the
rejecting gesture's alleged purpose is to thwart an oncoming
desire, it nevertheless appears *as a gesture*, thus *making itself
present* and lending itself to being read as a kind of offering or,
minimally, *presence*. Precisely because the gesture of rejection
is, it rhetorically denies the threat of withdrawal that it nevertheless purports to signify. For the infant, the presence or de-
terminacy of that object, no matter how persistently rejecting,
is nevertheless a site of presence and excitation and, hence, is
better than no object at all. This truism is not far from Nietzsche's line that the will would rather will nothingness than not
will at all. In both cases, the desire to desire is a willingness to
desire precisely that which would foreclose desire, if only for
the possibility of continuing to desire.

The question, then, that Hegel and Freud would appear to pose for Foucault is whether this terrain of "stubborn attachment" does not in some way figure in the scenarios of subjection that he describes. To what extent does a regulatory regime exploit this willingness to attach blindly to what seeks to suppress or negate that very attachment? And to what extent does the attachment that a regulatory regime requires prove to be both its constitutive failure and the potential site of resistance? If desire has as its final aim the continuation of itself—and here one might link Hegel, Freud, and Foucault all back to Spinoza's *conatus*—then the capacity of desire to be withdrawn and to reattach will constitute something like the vulnerability of every strategy of subjection.

2

Circuits of Bad Conscience

Nietzsche and Freud

Nietzsche offers a view of conscience as a mental activity that not only forms various psychic phenomena, but is itself *formed*, the consequence of a distinctive kind of internalization. In Nietzsche, who distinguishes conscience from bad conscience, the will is said to turn back upon itself. But what are we to make of this strange locution; how are we being asked to imagine a will such that it recoils and redoubles upon itself; and how, most pertinently, is this figure being offered as a way to articulate the kind of reflexivity central to the operation of bad conscience? Freud will use a similar language in writing of the formation of conscience, especially in relation to paranoia and narcissism. He describes conscience as the force of a desire—although sometimes a force of aggression—as it turns back on itself, and he understands prohibition, not as a law external to desire, but as the very operation of desire as it turns on its own possibility. What sense do we make of the figure that emerges in the context of both explanations, that of a will that turns back on itself, that of a desire that turns back on itself? We must ask not only how this figure of recoiling and

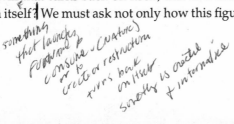

redoubling becomes central to understanding bad conscience, but what this figure suggests about the bodily position or disposition encoded in the structure of reflexivity. Why does a body doubled over on itself figure what it means to be a self-conscious sort of being? _contradicts nature_

The notion that morality is predicated on a certain kind of violence is already familiar, but more surprising is that such violence founds the subject. Morality performs that violence again and again in cultivating the subject as a reflexive being. This is, in part, what led Nietzsche to reflect that morality is a kind of illness. If this turning on oneself can be called a kind of violence, it cannot simply be opposed in the name of nonviolence, for when and where it is opposed, it is opposed from a position that presupposes this very violence. I do not wish simply to underscore the aporetic structure involved in the assumption of morality, nor simply to affirm the generalized violence in any and all moral positioning, although both insights, furnished by deconstruction, form a point of departure for what I seek to do. Rather, I would suggest that the subject who would oppose violence, even violence to itself, is itself the effect of a prior violence without which the subject could not have emerged. Can that particular circle be broken? How and when does that breakage occur? And what emerges as a significant possibility in which the subject loses its closed contour, the circularity of its own reflexive closure? A pure will, ontologically intact prior to any articulation, does not suddenly emerge as a principle of self-augmentation and self-affirmation that exceeds the bounds of any and all regulatory schemas. Rather, the formative and fabricating dimension of psychic life, which travels under the name of the "will," and which is usually associated with a restrictively aesthetic domain, proves central to refashioning the normative shackles that no subject can do without, but which no subject is condemned to repeat in exactly the same way.

My inquiry concerns a persistent problem that emerges when we try to think the possibility of a will that takes itself as its own object and, through the formation of that kind of reflexivity, binds itself to itself, acquires its own identity through reflexivity. To what extent is this apparent self-bondage fully or exclusively self-imposed? Is this strange posture of the will in the service of a social regulation that requires the production of the subject a consequence or an expression of bad conscience? I suppose that those who seek to redeem Nietzsche by claiming that he can be invoked in the service of the ethical might think that the only alternative worse than bad conscience is its obliteration. But remember that Nietzsche not only distinguishes between the ethical and morality, but asks about the *value* of morality, thus instating a value by which morality might be assessed, but suggesting as well that this assessment, this valuation, may not be reducible to morality.

I take it that the juxtaposition of Nietzsche with the question of ethics is, indeed, a question because Nietzsche and various figures within the Continental tradition have been found guilty by association with irresponsible acts and events. What will be the response to these charges? To take the side of the ethical, to relate each and every thinker to the ethical? Or will this be an occasion to think the problem a bit more carefully, to continue to pose the ethical as a question, one which cannot be freed of its complicity with what it most strongly opposes? Will this, paradoxically, become a time in which we reflect upon the more pervasive dimensions of complicity and what might be derived from such a vexed relation to power?

I understand the desire to resituate Nietzsche within the ethical domain as an effort to counter the caricature, within contemporary criticism, of Nietzsche as one who only destroys the domain of values (where that destruction is not itself a source of value, or a value in itself). I want instead to suggest that Nietzsche offers us a political insight into the formation of the psyche and the problem of subjection, understood paradoxically not merely as the subordination of a subject to a norm, but as the constitution of a subject through precisely such a subordination. Indeed, to the extent that bad conscience involves a turning against oneself, a body in recoil upon itself, how does this figure serve the social regulation of the subject, and how might we understand this more fundamental subjection, without which no proper subject emerges? I want to suggest that, although there is no final undoing of the reflexive bind, that posture of the self bent against itself, a passionate deregulation of the subject may perhaps precipitate a tenuous unraveling of that constitutive knot. What emerges is not the unshackled will or a "beyond" to power, but another direction for what is most formative in passion, a formative power which is at once the condition of its violence against itself, its status as a necessary fiction, and the site of its enabling possibilities. This recasting of the "will" is not, properly speaking, the will of a subject, nor is it an effect fully cultivated by and through social norms; it is, I would suggest, the site at which the social implicates the psychic in its very formation—or, to be more precise, *as* its very formation and formativity.

Consider the general claim that the social regulation of the subject compels a passionate attachment to regulation, and that this formation of the will takes place in part through the action of a repression. Although one is tempted to claim that social regulation is simply internalized, taken from the outside and brought into the psyche, the problem is more complicated and, indeed, more insidious. For the boundary that divides the outside from the inside is in the process of being installed, precisely through the regulation of the subject. The repression is the very turning back on itself which the passionate attachment to subjection performs. How can a will be enticed to make such a turn? Are we to think that turn as an internal bending of the psyche against itself? If so, why is it figured as a body that turns on and against itself? Are the psychic and the somatic articulated through one another in such a way that the figuration of the first is implicated invariably in a chiastic relation to the second? Clearly, what is at stake is something more than and different from a relation between an external demand offered by regulatory power and an internal recoil registered as its secondary effect. If presupposed in the very notion of the subject is a passionate attachment to subjection, then the subject will not emerge save as an exemplification and effect of this attachment. I hope to show, first through a consideration of Nietzsche, then in relation to Freud, how the very notion of reflexivity, as an emergent structure of the subject, is the consequence of a "turning back on itself," a repeated self-beratement which comes to form the misnomer of "conscience," and that there is no formation of the subject without a passionate attachment to subjection.

Significantly, Nietzsche attributes a creative or formative power to conscience, and the act of turning back upon oneself is not only the condition of the possibility of the subject, but the condition of the possibility of fiction, fabrication, and transfiguration. Indeed, Nietzsche remarks that bad conscience *fabricates* the soul, that expanse of interior psychic space. If the subject is understood as a kind of necessary fiction, then it is also one of the first artistic accomplishments presupposed by morality. The artistic accomplishments of bad conscience exceed the purview of the subject; indeed, they will come to include "all imaginative and ideal phenomena," including conceptual thinking, figurative writing, and the conjectured fables and myths which compose the various retrospective imaginings of genealogy. In this sense, the condition of possibility of Nietzsche's own writing appears to be the bad conscience for which it seeks to give an account.

Nietzsche offers a narrative that seeks to account for this formation, but his narrative will be afflicted from the start by the very conscience that it seeks to uncover for us. The claim that conscience is a fiction is not to be confused with the claim that conscience is arbitrary or dispensable; on the contrary, it is a necessary fiction, one without which the grammatical and phenomenological subject cannot exist. But if its fictive status does not dispel its necessity, how are we to construe the sense of that necessity? More precisely, what does it mean to say that a subject emerges only through the action of turning back on itself? If this turning back on oneself is a trope, a movement which is always and only *figured* as a bodily movement, but which no body literally performs, in what will the necessity of such a figuration consist? The trope appears to be the shadow of a body, a shadowing of that body's violence against itself, a body in spectral and linguistic form that is the signifying mark of the psyche's emergence.

Considered grammatically, it will seem that there must first be a subject who turns back on itself, yet I will argue that there is no subject except as a consequence of this very reflexivity. How can the subject be presumed at both ends of this process, especially when it is the very formation of the subject for which this process seeks to give an account?

If, in Freud, conscience is a passionate attachment to *prohibition*, an attachment which takes the form of a turning back on oneself, does the formation of the ego take place as the sedimented result of this peculiar form of reflexivity? The noun form "ego" will then reify and mask the iterated accumulation of this reflexive movement. Of what is this reflexivity composed? What is it that is said to turn back upon what? And what composes the action of "turning back upon"? I want to suggest that this logical circularity in which the subject appears at once to be presupposed and not yet formed, on the one hand, or formed and hence not presupposed, on the other, is ameliorated when one understands that in both Freud and Nietzsche this relationship of reflexivity is always and only figured, and that this figure makes no ontological claim. To refer to a "will," much less to its "turning back on itself," is a strange way to speak, strange because it figures a process which cannot be detached from or understood apart from that very figuration. Indeed, for Nietzsche, the writing of such figurations, and figuration in general, are part and parcel of the "ideal and imaginative phenomena" which are the consequences of bad conscience. Hence, we do not come to know something about bad conscience when we consider the strange figure of reflexivity that Nietzsche offers us. We are, as it were, caught up in the luring effects of bad conscience at the very textual moment when we seek to know what, precisely, this bad conscience is. If it is credited with being the ground of figuration, yet can itself only be figured—indeed, figured *as* that ground—the circularity which might be lamented from a logical perspective concerned with establishing clear sequence becomes the constitutive feature of bad conscience, considered both as a figure and as the condition of possibility for figuration itself.

The apparent circularity of this account reappears in a related set of quandaries. What motivates the will to turn back on itself? Does it turn back on itself under the pressure of an external force or law, under the anticipated or recollected force of punishment? Or does this peculiar form of reflexivity take place prior to, or in some other form of complicity with, a set of externally imposed demands?

To clarify this last point it is important to reconsider the thesis that punishment precedes conscience, and that conscience can be understood as the unproblematic internalization of punishment, its mnemonic trace. Although there are clearly textual moments in which Nietzsche appears to be arguing for such a temporal priority of punishment to conscience, there are also competing views in Nietzsche which call this sequential account into question.

If the will in Nietzsche is at its most productive—that is, its most conscientious—when it is turned back upon itself, then it appears that the severity of conscience is linked to the strength of the will of which it is composed. Similarly, for Freud, the strength of conscience is nourished precisely by the aggression that it forbids. In this sense, then, the strength of conscience correlates neither with the strength of a punishment received nor with the strength of a memory of a punishment received, *but with the strength of one's own aggression*, one which is said to have vented itself externally, but which now, under the rubric of bad conscience, is said to vent itself internally. This latter venting is also at the same time a fabricating: an internalization which is produced or fabricated as the effect of a sublimation.

This circularity appears to break the line of causality or internalization usually conjectured between an external or historical experience of punishment and an internalization of the mnemonic trace of that punishment in the form of conscience. But if conscience is self-derived in this way, and not derived unilaterally from an internalization of an external or historical punishment, is there some other way to understand its function in the process of social regulation? Is it possible to understand the force of punishment outside of the ways in which it exploits a narcissistic demand, or, to put it in a Nietzschean vein, is it possible to understand the force of punishment outside of the ways in which it exploits the will's attachment to itself?

To claim that there is a passionate attachment to subjection appears to presuppose that there is first a passion, and that its aim is to attach to some kind of object. In Nietzsche, there will emerge a question of whether this primary passion, this will, precedes the attachments by which it is known, or whether its attachments precede its passions or acquire their passionate character only after an attachment is assumed. (It may invariably be both, participating in an incommensurable set of temporal trajectories. In some ways, we might see this question as pervading the debates between Lacanian and object-relations construals of Freud.)

Nietzsche's Account of Bad Conscience

Nietzsche's consideration of bad conscience in *On the Genealogy of Morals* is introduced in section 16 of the second essay. At first, the relation of this notion to the notion of conscience introduced earlier in the same essay is unclear. Conscience is introduced via the animal who is bred to keep promises, and in relation to the "sovereign" man. The one who makes and keeps his promise is one who "has bred in himself a . . . faculty" opposed to forgetfulness, namely, a memory, which becomes "a *memory of the will*."[1] Here Nietzsche refers to an "impression" that is actively sustained by a desire, one which is not forgotten, but which, in being actively remembered, produces the protracted continuity of the will. But this impression is not specified. An impression from where? In the service of what? Nietzsche then insists that the one who makes promises will not allow anything to interrupt the process by which an original statement, "I will" or "I shall do this," culminates in the discharge of the designated act. The one who truly promises wields the power of the sovereign to enact what he says, to bring into being what he wills. In other words, the promising being establishes a continuity between a statement and an act, although the temporal disjunction between the two is acknowledged as an opportunity for the intervention of various competing circumstances and accidents. In the face of these circumstances and accidents, the will continues to produce itself, to labor on itself in the service of making of itself a continuity, where that continuity, that "long chain of will," as Nietzsche puts it, establishes its own temporality over and against any other which might seek to complicate or qualify its execution. This promising being is one who stands for himself through time and whose word continues through time, one "who gives [his] word as something that can be relied on because [h]e know[s] himself to be strong enough to maintain it in the face of accidents" (60/294). This protracted will, which is self-identical through time and which establishes its own time, constitutes the man of conscience. (Oddly enough, this ideal of the efficacious speech act presupposed by promising is undercut by Nietzsche's own notion of the sign chain, according to which a sign is bound to signify in ways that estrange the sign from the originating intentions by which it is mobilized. According to the historicity of the sign chain, it would be impossible to keep a promise, because it would be impossible to safeguard a sign from the various historical accidents by which its meaning is augmented in excess of its originating intentions.)

In section 3, which follows this discussion, Nietzsche reconsiders this idealization of the promising animal and asks how a memory can be created for a will. This returns us to the question concerning the status of the "impression" that is actively reanimated and relived, and which, in and through its reanimation, establishes the protracted continuity of the will. "If something is to stay in the memory, it must be burned in; only that which never ceases to *hurt* stays in the memory" (61/295). And we then learn of the "terror" that formerly attended all promises. Is this "terror," then, to be construed as the "impression" that works as the mnemonic device whereby the will makes itself regular and calculable? By section 4, Nietzsche poses the question of bad conscience explicitly, but continues to treat it as if it were quite separate from conscience itself. He asks: How did "that other 'somber thing,' the consciousness of guilt, the 'bad conscience,' come into the world?" (62/297). But is it *other*? Is there a way for the will to become regular, to become the protracted continuity which underwrites the promise, without becoming subject to the logic of bad conscience?

Well-known discussions of the relation between debt and guilt follow (62–63/297–98), in which the failure to repay a loan awakens the desire for compensation in the creditor, and injury is inflicted on the debtor. The attribution of moral accountability to the debtor thus rationalizes the desire of the creditor to punish the debtor. With that notion of "accountability" emerges a whole panoply of morally saturated psychic phenomena: intentionality, even certain versions of the will itself. But the desire to punish cannot be fully accounted for by the circumstances of the broken contract. Why does the creditor take pleasure in the infliction of injury, and what form does that pleasure take when injury is inflicted in the moralized action by which the creditor holds the debtor morally accountable and pronounces him guilty? What strange consummation of pleasure takes place in that attribution of guilt?

   This account of how the attribution of guilt originates is not
yet the formation of bad conscience (which would, of course,
be the self-attribution or self-infliction of guilt). It presupposes that a contract has been broken, and the existence of the
contract presupposes the institution of promising. Indeed, the
debtor is one who fails to keep his promise, protract his will,
and discharge his word in the execution of an act.

   The punishment of the debtor thus presupposes the model
or ideal of the promising animal, yet this promising animal
could not come into being without the impressions of terror
produced by punishment. The punishment of the debtor appears to emerge in response to an injury, the debt being cast
as that injury, but the response takes on a meaning that exceeds the explicit purpose of achieving compensation. For the
punishment is pleasurable, and the infliction of injury is construed as a seduction to life (66–67/301–2).

   If this complicated scene animates the creditor, how do we
understand the formation of bad conscience in the debtor?
Nietzsche writes, "Punishment is supposed to have the value
of awakening the feeling of guilt in the guilty person; one
seeks in it the actual *instrumentum* of that psychical reaction
called 'bad conscience,' 'sting of conscience' " (81/318).

   But Nietzsche takes his distance from this formulation,
since not merely psychic reactions, but the psyche itself is
the instrument of this punishment. The internalization of instinct—which takes place when the instinct does not immediately discharge as the deed—is understood to produce the soul
or the psyche instead; the pressure exerted from the walls of
society forces an internalization which culminates in the production of the soul, this production being understood as a primary artistic accomplishment, the fabrication of an ideal. This
fabrication appears to take the place of the promise, the word

actualized as deed, and to emerge on the condition that the promise has been broken. But recall that the execution of the deed was not without its fabrications: one effect of the promise is to produce an "I" which might stand for itself across time. Thus, the fabrication of such an "I" is the paradoxical result of the promise. The "I" becomes continuous with its deed, but its deed is, paradoxically, to create the continuity of itself.

Bad conscience would be the fabrication of interiority that attends the breaking of a promise, the discontinuity of the will, but the "I" who would keep the promise is precisely the cultivated effect of this continuous fabrication of interiority. Can there even be a promising being, one who is able to discharge words into deeds, without the bad conscience which forms the very "I" who makes good his word through time, who has a memory of the will, and for whom the psyche has already been produced?

Nietzsche describes "bad conscience in its beginnings" as the *"instinct for freedom* forcibly made latent" (87/325). But where is the trace of this freedom in the self-shackling that Nietzsche describes? It is to be found in the pleasure taken in afflicting pain, a pleasure taken in afflicting pain on oneself in the service of, in the name of, morality. This pleasure in affliction, attributed earlier to the creditor, thus becomes, under the pressure of the social contract, an internalized pleasure, the joy of persecuting oneself. The origin of bad conscience is, thus, the joy taken in persecuting oneself, where the self persecuted does not exist outside the orbit of that persecution. But the internalization of punishment is the very production of the self, and it is in this production that pleasure and freedom are curiously located. Punishment is not merely productive of the self, but this very productivity of punishment is the site for the freedom and pleasure of the will, its fabricating activity.

As a peculiar deformation of artistry (which is, of course, indistinguishable from its primary formation), self-consciousness is the form the will takes when it is prevented from simple expression as a deed. But is the model by which an instinct or a will expresses or discharges itself in a deed in any sense prior to this self-thwarted expression of bad conscience? Can there be a model of promising that does not from the first presuppose bad conscience? The noble is described earlier as one for whom his work is "an instinctive creation and imposition of forms . . . the most involuntary and unconscious artists [that] there are" (86/325). The soul is precisely what a certain violent artistry produces when it takes itself as its own object. The soul, the psyche, is not there prior to this reflexive move, but this reflexive turning of the will against itself produces in its wake the metaphorics of psychic life.

If we understand the soul to be the effect of imposing a form upon oneself, where the form is taken to be equivalent to the soul, then there can be no protracted will, no "I" that stands for itself through time, without this self-imposition of form, this moral laboring on oneself. This fundamentally artistic production of bad conscience, the production of a "form" from and of the will, is described by Nietzsche as "the womb of all ideal and imaginative phenomena" (87/326). Bad conscience is fabricated, but it in turn is credited with the fabrication of all ideal and imaginative phenomena. Is there, then, any way to answer the question of whether artistry precedes bad conscience or is its result? Is there any way to postulate something before this "turning back upon itself" which is the tropic foundation of the subject and all artistry, including all imagination and conceptual life?

If bad conscience *originates* imaginative and ideal phenomena, then it is difficult to imagine which of Nietzsche's fabulous genealogical terms would not finally be attributable to this bad conscience. Indeed, his project of offering a genealogy of bad conscience appears to founder when the very terms he will use to account for this formation turn out to be the effect of this formation itself. Elsewhere he will refuse, for instance, to accept the notion of the will as a conceptual given. In *Beyond Good and Evil*, he writes, "willing seems to me to be . . . something *complicated*, something that is a unit only as a word."[2] Once willing is elevated to the status of a philosophical concept, he writes, it is of necessity a kind of fiction. The same would clearly hold for the notion of "instinct," and also for the effort to account chronologically or sequentially for how anything can be derived from the will, or the will from anything else: "one should use 'cause' and 'effect' only as pure concepts, that is to say, as conventional fictions for the purpose of designation and communication—*not* for explanation."[3] In *On the Genealogy of Morals*, he reiterates that conceptualization emerges from the genealogy of torture as the promise of a certain escape: concepts, he writes, are an effort to gain release from a torture. Is the very conceptual apparatus of *On the Genealogy of Morals* implicated in this description, and is Nietzsche's text then an effort to escape from the tortures of bad conscience, although it owes its life, as it were, to that very source?

If all "imaginative phenomena" are the result of this violent interiorization, it follows that the genealogical account will be one of these phenomena, a narrative effect of the narrative it seeks to tell. The unmasking of the narrative is its remasking— inevitably. Indeed, it seems that the very creativity one seeks to oppose to the inhibition of strength is fundamentally dependent on that very inhibition. In this sense, repression appears to underwrite or guarantee both the being who promises and the writer of fiction, including conceptual fictions such as genealogy. The unity of will attributed to the promising is itself the *effect* of a repression, a forgetfulness, a not-remembering of the satisfactions which appear to precede repression, and which repression makes sure will not appear again.

Freud, Narcissism, and Regulation

In this final section, I would like to return to the problem of social regulation, not as acting on a psyche, but as complicitous in the formation of the psyche and its desire. To that end, I propose a detour through Freud; the Nietzschean resonances in his consideration of conscience will become clear.

The postulation of repression's primacy brings us directly to Freud, and to a reconsideration of the problem of punishment in relation to the formation of conscience and social subjection. If this subjection is not mechanistic, not the simple effect of an internalization, then how can we understand the psychic engagement with subjection in a way that does not disjoin the discourse of self-subjection from the problem of social regulation? How can cultivating a narcissistic attachment to punishment be the means by which the power of social regulation exploits a narcissistic demand for self-reflection which is indifferent to its occasion?

This suggestion of narcissism is, I would suggest, already at work in Nietzsche. The ascetic ideal, understood as a will to nothingness, is a way of interpreting all suffering as guilt. Whereas guilt works to deny a specific kind of object for human wants, it cannot obliterate the wanting character of humans. According to the dictates of guilt, then, "man had only to *want* something—and to begin with, it mattered not what, whereto, or how he wanted: *the will itself was saved"* (162/411).

In his analysis of neurosis, Freud understood this differently, as a kind of libidinal attachment to a prohibition which has as its purpose the thwarting of libidinal gratification. Where that thwarting constitutes a repression, the repression is sustained by the libido that it seeks to thwart. In neurosis, the ethical regulation of bodily impulse becomes the focus and aim of impulse itself. Here we are given to understand an attachment to subjection which is formative of the reflexive structure of subjection. The impulse which would be negated is inadvertently *preserved* by that very negating activity.

We can hear a resonance of Nietzsche when Freud describes the process by which libido comes under the censor of the law only to reemerge as the sustaining affect of that law. The repression of the libido is always to be understood as itself a libidinally invested repression. Hence, the libido is not absolutely negated through repression, but rather becomes the instrument of its own subjection. The repressive law is not external to the libido that it represses, but the repressive law represses to the extent that repression becomes a libidinal activity. Further, moral interdictions, especially those that are turned against the body, are themselves sustained by the bodily activity that they seek to curb.

The desire to desire is a willingness to desire precisely what would foreclose desire, if only for the possibility of continuing to desire. This desire for desire is exploited in the process of social regulation, for if the terms by which we gain social recognition for ourselves are those by which we are regulated *and* gain social existence, then to affirm one's existence is to capitulate to one's subordination—a sorry bind. How precisely this narcissistic attachment to attachment is exploited by mechanisms of social regulation is inadvertently made clear in a set of speculations that Freud offers on the repression of homosexuality and the formation of conscience and citizenship. In "On the Mechanism of Paranoia," he links the suppression of homosexual drives to the production of social feeling. At the end of that piece, he remarks that "homosexual drives" help to constitute "the social instincts, thus contributing an erotic factor to friendship and comradeship, to *esprit de corps* and to the love of mankind in general."[4] At the close of the essay "On Narcissism," he might be read as specifying the logic whereby this production of social feeling takes place. The "ego-ideal," he writes, has a social side: "it is also the common ideal of a family, a class or a nation. It not only binds the narcissistic libido, but also a considerable amount of the person's homosexual libido, which in this way becomes turned back into the ego. The dissatisfaction due to the non-fulfillment of the ideal liberates homosexual libido, which is transformed into sense of guilt (dread of the community)."[5] This transformation of homosexuality into guilt and, therefore, into the basis of social feeling takes place when the fear of parental punishment becomes generalized as the dread of losing the love of fellow men. Paranoia is the way in which that love is consistently reimagined as always almost withdrawn, and it is, paradoxically, fear of losing that love which motivates the sublimation or introversion of homosexuality. Indeed, this sublimation is not quite as instrumental as it may sound, for it is not that one disavows homosexuality in order to gain the love of fellow men, but that a certain homosexuality can only be achieved and contained *through* this disavowal.

Another place in Freud where this becomes very clear is the discussion of the formation of conscience in *Civilization and*

Its Discontents, where it turns out that the prohibition against homosexuality which conscience is said to enact or articulate founds and constitutes conscience itself as a psychic phenomenon. The prohibition against the desire is that desire as it turns back upon itself, and this turning back upon itself becomes the very inception, the very action of what is rendered entitative through the term "conscience."

Freud writes in *Civilization and Its Discontents* "that conscience (or more correctly, the anxiety which later becomes conscience) is indeed the cause of instinctual renunciation to begin with, but that later the relationship is reversed. Every renunciation of instinct now becomes a dynamic source of conscience and every fresh renunciation increases the latter's severity and intolerance."[6]

According to Freud, then, the self-imposed imperatives that characterize the circular route of conscience are pursued and applied precisely because they are now the site of the very satisfaction that they seek to prohibit. In other words, prohibition becomes the occasion for reliving the instinct under the rubric of the condemning law. Prohibition reproduces the prohibited desire and becomes intensified through the renunciations it effects. The "afterlife" of prohibited desire takes place through the prohibition itself, where the prohibition not only sustains, but is *sustained by* the desire that it forces into renunciation. In this sense, then, renunciation takes place through the very desire that is renounced: the desire is *never* renounced, but becomes preserved and reasserted in the very structure of renunciation.

This example leads us back to the trope with which we began, the figure of conscience as turning back on itself as if it were a body recoiled on itself, recoiled at the thought of its desire, for whom its desire is symptomatized as that posture of recoil. Conscience is thus figured as a body which takes itself as its object, forced into a permanent posture of negative narcissism or, more precisely, a narcissistically nourished self-beratement (then, mistakenly, identified with a narcissistic *stage*).

Consider—as a parting shot—how the contemporary efforts to regulate homosexuality within the U.S. military are themselves the regulatory formation of the masculine subject, one who consecrates his identity through *renunciation* as an act of speech: to say "I am a homosexual" is fine as long as one also *promises* "and I don't intend to act." This, the suppression and sustaining of homosexuality in and through the circular posture by which a body utters its own renunciation, accedes to its regulation through the promise. But that performative utterance, however compelled, will be subject to infelicity, to speaking otherwise, to reciting only half the sentence, deforming the promise, reformulating the confession as defiance, remaining silent. This opposition will draw from and oppose the power by which it is compelled, and this short circuiting of regulatory power constitutes the possibility of a *postmoral* gesture toward a less regular freedom, one that from the perspective of a less codifiable set of values calls into question the values of morality.

Subjection, Resistance, Resignification

Between Freud and Foucault

My problem is essentially the definition of the implicit
systems in which we find ourselves prisoners; what I would
like to grasp is the system of limits and exclusion which
we practice without knowing it; I would like to make the
cultural unconscious apparent.
                    —Foucault, "Rituals of Exclusion"

Consider, in *Discipline and Punish*, the paradoxical character of what Foucault describes as the subjectivation of
the prisoner. The term "subjectivation" carries the paradox in
itself: *assujetissement* denotes both the becoming of the subject
and the process of subjection—one inhabits the figure of autonomy only by becoming subjected to a power, a subjection
which implies a radical dependency. For Foucault, this process of subjectivation takes place centrally through the body.
In *Discipline and Punish* the prisoner's body not only appears
as a *sign* of guilt and transgression, as the embodiment of prohibition and the sanction for rituals of normalization, but is

framed and formed through the discursive matrix of a juridical subject. The claim that a discourse "forms" the body is no simple one, and from the start we must distinguish how such "forming" is not the same as a "causing" or "determining," still less is it a notion that bodies are somehow made of discourse pure and simple.[1]

Foucault suggests that the prisoner is not regulated by an *exterior* relation of power, whereby an institution takes a pregiven individual as the target of its subordinating aims. On the contrary, the individual is formed or, rather, formulated through his discursively constituted "identity" as prisoner. Subjection is, literally, the *making* of a subject, the principle of regulation according to which a subject is formulated or produced. Such subjection is a kind of power that not only unilaterally *acts on* a given individual as a form of domination, but also *activates* or forms the subject. Hence, subjection is neither simply the domination of a subject nor its production, but designates a certain kind of restriction *in* production, a restriction without which the production of the subject cannot take place, a restriction through which that production takes place. Although Foucault occasionally tries to argue that historically *juridical* power—power acting on, subordinating, pregiven subjects—*precedes* productive power, the capacity of power to *form* subjects, with the prisoner it is clear that the subject produced and the subject regulated or subordinated are one, and that compulsory production is its own form of regulation.

Foucault warns against those within the liberal tradition who would liberate the prisoner from the prison's oppressive confines, for the subjection signified by the exterior institution of the prison does not act apart from the invasion and management of the prisoner's body: what Foucault describes as the full siege and invasion of that body by the signifying practices of the prison—namely, inspection, confession, the regularization and normalization of bodily movement and gesture, the disciplinary regimes of the body which have led feminists to consult Foucault in order to elaborate the disciplinary production of gender.[2] The prison thus acts on the prisoner's body, but it does so by forcing the prisoner to approximate an ideal, a norm of behavior, a model of obedience. This is how the prisoner's individuality is rendered coherent, totalized, made into the discursive and conceptual possession of the prison; it is, as Foucault insists, the way in which "he becomes the principle of his own subjection."[3] This normative ideal inculcated, as it were, into the prisoner is a kind of psychic identity, or what Foucault will call a "soul." Because the soul is an imprisoning effect, Foucault claims that the prisoner is subjected "in a more fundamental way" than by the spatial captivity of the prison. Indeed, in the citation that follows, the soul is figured as itself a kind of spatial captivity, indeed, as a kind of prison, which provides the exterior form or regulatory principle of the prisoner's body. This becomes clear in Foucault's formulation that "the man described for us, whom we are invited to free, is already in himself the effect of a subjection [*assujettisse-ment*] much more profound than himself . . . the soul is the prison of the body" (30).

Although Foucault is specifying the subjectivation of the prisoner here, he appears also to be privileging the metaphor of the prison to theorize the subjectivation of the body. What are we to make of imprisonment and invasion as the privileged figures through which Foucault articulates the process of subjectivation, the discursive production of identities? If discourse produces identity by supplying and enforcing a regulatory principle which thoroughly invades, totalizes, and renders coherent the individual, then it seems that every "identity," insofar as it is totalizing, acts as precisely such a "soul that imprisons the body." In what sense is this soul "much more profound" than the prisoner himself? Does this mean that the soul preexists the body that animates it? How are we to understand such a claim in the context of Foucault's theory of power?

Rather than answer that question directly, one might for the purposes of clarification counterpose the "soul," which Foucault articulates as an imprisoning frame, to the psyche in the psychoanalytic sense.[4] In the psyche, the subject's ideal corresponds to the ego-ideal, which the super-ego is said to consult, as it were, in order to measure the ego. Lacan redescribes this ideal as the "position" of the subject within the symbolic, the norm that installs the subject within language and hence within available schemes of cultural intelligibility. This viable and intelligible being, this subject, is always produced at a cost, and whatever resists the normative demand by which subjects are instituted remains unconscious. Thus the psyche, which includes the unconscious, is very different from the subject: the psyche is precisely what exceeds the imprisoning effects of the discursive demand to inhabit a coherent identity, to become a coherent subject. The psyche is what resists the regularization that Foucault ascribes to normalizing discourses. Those discourses are said to imprison the body *in the soul*, to animate and contain the body within that ideal frame, and to that extent reduce the notion of the psyche to the operations of an externally framing and normalizing ideal.[5] This Foucaultian move appears to treat the psyche as if it received unilaterally the effect of the Lacanian symbolic. The transposition of the soul into an exterior and imprisoning frame for the body vacates, as it were, the interiority of the body, leaving that interiority as a malleable surface for the unilateral effects of disciplinary power.

I am in part moving toward a psychoanalytic criticism of Foucault, for I think that one cannot account for subjectivation and, in particular, becoming the principle of one's own subjection without recourse to a psychoanalytic account of the formative or generative effects of restriction or prohibition. Moreover, the formation of the subject cannot fully be thought —if it ever can be—without recourse to a paradoxically enabling set of grounding constraints. Yet as I elaborate this critique, some romanticized notions of the unconscious defined as necessary resistance will come under critical scrutiny, and that criticism will entail the reemergence of a Foucaultian perspective *within* psychoanalysis. The question of a suppressed psychoanalysis in Foucault—raised by Foucault himself in the reference to a "cultural unconscious" quoted in the epigraph to this chapter—might be raised more precisely as the problem of locating or accounting for resistance. Where does resistance to or in disciplinary subject formation take place? Does the reduction of the psychoanalytically rich notion of the psyche to that of the imprisoning soul eliminate the possibility of resistance to normalization and to subject formation, a resistance that emerges precisely from the incommensurability between psyche and subject? How would we understand such resistance, and would such an understanding entail a critical rethinking of psychoanalysis along the way?

In what follows, I will ask two different kinds of questions, one of Foucault, and another of psychoanalysis (applying this term variously to Freud and to Lacan).[6] First, if Foucault understands the psyche to be an imprisoning effect in the service of normalization, then how might he account for psychic resistance to normalization? Second, when some proponents of psychoanalysis insist that resistance to normalization is a function of the unconscious, is this guarantee of psychic resistance merely sleight of hand? More precisely, is the resistance upon which psychoanalysis insists socially and discursively produced, or is it a kind of resistance to, an undermining of, social and discursive production *as such*? Consider the claim that the unconscious only and always resists normalization, that every ritual of conformity to the injunctions of civilization comes at a cost, and that a certain unharnessed and unsocialized remainder is thereby produced, which contests the appearance of the law-abiding subject. This psychic remainder signifies the limits of normalization. That position does not imply that such resistance wields the power to rework or rearticulate the terms of discursive demand, the disciplinary injunctions by which normalization occurs. To thwart the injunction to produce a docile body is not the same as dismantling the injunction or changing the terms of subject constitution. If the unconscious, or the psyche more generally, is defined as resistance, what do we then make of unconscious attachments to subjection, which imply that the unconscious is no more free of normalizing discourse than the subject? If the unconscious escapes from a given normative injunction, to what other injunction does it form an attachment? What makes us think that the unconscious is any less structured by the power relations that pervade cultural signifiers than is the language of the subject? If we find an attachment to subjection at the level of the unconscious, what kind of resistance is to be wrought from that?

Even if we grant that unconscious resistance to a normalizing injunction guarantees the failure of that injunction fully to constitute its subject, does such resistance do anything to alter or expand the dominant injunctions or interpellations of subject formation? What do we make of a resistance that can only undermine, but which appears to have no power to re-articulate the terms, the symbolic terms—to use Lacanian par-lance—by which subjects are constituted, by which subjection is installed in the very formation of the subject? This resistance establishes the incomplete character of any effort to produce a subject by disciplinary means, but it remains unable to re-articulate the dominant terms of productive power.

Before continuing this interrogation of psychoanalysis, however, let us return to the problem of bodies in Foucault. How and why is resistance denied to bodies produced through disciplinary regimes? What is this notion of disciplinary pro-duction, and does it work as efficaciously as Foucault appears to imply? In the final chapter of the first volume of *The His-tory of Sexuality*, Foucault calls for a "history of bodies" which would inquire into "the manner in which what is most ma-terial and vital in them has been invested."[7] In this formula-tion, he suggests that power acts not only *on* the body but also *in* the body, that power not only produces the boundaries of a subject but pervades the interiority of that subject. In the last formulation, it appears that there is an "inside" to the body which exists before power's invasion. But given the radical ex-teriority of the soul, how are we to understand "interiority" in Foucault?[8] That interiority will not be a soul, and it will not be a psyche, but what will it be? Is this a space of pure malleability, one which is, as it were, ready to conform to the demands of socialization? Or is this interiority to be called, simply, the body? Has it come to the paradoxical point where Foucault wants to claim that the soul is the exterior form, and the body the interior space?

Although Foucault wants on occasion to refute the possi-bility of a body which is not produced through power rela-tions, sometimes his explanations require a body to maintain a materiality ontologically distinct from the power relations that take it as a site of investment.[9] Indeed, the term "site" seemingly appears in this phrase without warrant, for what is the relation between the body as *site* and the investments which that site is said to receive or bear? Does the term "site" stabilize the body in relation to those investments, while deflecting the question of how investments establish, contour, and disrupt what the phrase takes for granted as the body's "site" (i.e., does the term "site" deflect the project of Lacan's "mirror stage")? What constitutes an "investment," and what is its constituting power? Does it have a visualizing function, and can we understand the production of the bodily ego in Freud as the projected or spatialized modality of such investments?[10] Indeed, to what extent is the body's site stabilized through a certain projective instability, one which Foucault cannot quite describe and which would perhaps engage him in the problematic of the ego as an imaginary function?

Discipline and Punish offers a different configuration of the relation between materiality and investment. There the soul is taken to be an instrument of power through which the body is cultivated and formed. In a sense, it acts as a power-laden schema that produces and actualizes the body. We can understand Foucault's references to the soul as an implicit reworking of the Aristotelian formulation in which the soul is understood to be the form and principle of the body's matter.[11] Foucault argues in *Discipline and Punish* that the soul becomes a normative and normalizing ideal according to which the body is trained, shaped, cultivated, and invested; it is a historically specific imaginary ideal (*idéal speculatif*) under which the body is materialized.

This "subjection" or *assujetissement* is not only a subordination but a securing and maintaining, a putting into place of a subject, a subjectivation. The "soul brings [the prisoner] to existence"; not unlike in Aristotle, the soul, as an instrument of power, forms and frames the body, stamps it, and in stamping it, brings it into being. In this formulation, there is no body outside of power, for the materiality of the body—indeed, materiality itself—is produced by and in direct relation to the investment of power. The materiality of the prison, Foucault writes, is established to the extent that (*dans la mésure ou*) it is a vector and instrument of power.[12] Hence, the prison is *materialized* to the extent that it is *invested with power*. To be grammatically accurate, there is no prison prior to its materialization; its materialization is coextensive with its investiture with power relations; and materiality is the effect and gauge of this investment. The prison comes to be only within the field of power relations, more specifically, only to the extent that it is saturated with such relations and that such a saturation is formative of its very being. Here the body—of the prisoner and of the prison—is not an independent materiality, a static surface or site, which a subsequent investment comes to mark, signify upon, or pervade; the body is that for which materialization and investiture are coextensive.

Although the soul is understood to frame the body in *Discipline and Punish*, Foucault suggests that the production of the "subject" takes place to some degree through the subordination and even destruction of the body. In "Nietzsche, Genealogy, History," Foucault remarks that only through the destruction of the body does the subject as a "dissociated unity" appear: "the body is the inscribed surface of events (traced by language and dissolved by ideas), the locus of a dissociated self (adopting the illusion of a substantial unity), and a volume in perpetual disintegration."[13] The subject appears at the expense of the body, an appearance conditioned in inverse relation to the disappearance of the body. The subject not only effectively takes the place of the body but acts as the soul which frames and forms the body in captivity. Here the forming and framing function of that exterior soul works against the body; indeed, it might be understood as the sublimation of the body in consequence of displacement and substitution.

In thus redescribing the body in Foucault, I have clearly wandered into a psychoanalytic vocabulary of sublimation. While there, let me pose a question to return to the issue of subjection and resistance. If the body is subordinated and to some extent destroyed as the dissociated self emerges, and if that emergence might be read as the sublimation of the body and the self be read as the body's ghostly form, then is there some part of the body which is not preserved in sublimation, some part of the body which remains unsublimated?

This bodily remainder, I would suggest, survives for such a subject in the mode of already, if not always, having been destroyed, in a kind of constitutive loss. The body is not a site on which a construction takes place; it is a destruction on the occasion of which a subject is formed. The formation of this subject is at once the framing, subordination, and regulation of the body, and the mode in which that destruction is preserved (in the sense of sustained and embalmed) *in* normalization.

If, then, the body is now to be understood as that which not only constitutes the subject in its dissociated and sublimated state, but also exceeds or resists any effort at sublimation, how are we to understand this body that is, as it were, negated or repressed so that the subject might live? One might expect the body to return in a non-normalizable wildness, and there are of course moments in Foucault when something like that happens. But more often than not, in Foucault the possibility of subversion or resistance appears (a) in the course of a subjectivation that exceeds the normalizing aims by which it is mobilized, for example, in "reverse-discourse," or (b) through convergence with other discursive regimes, whereby inadvertently produced discursive complexity undermines the teleological aims of normalization.[14] Thus resistance appears as the effect of power, as a part of power, its self-subversion.

In the theorization of resistance, a certain problem arises which concerns psychoanalysis and, by implication, the limits of subjectivation. For Foucault, the subject who is produced through subjection is not produced at an instant in its totality. Instead, it is in the process of being produced, it is repeatedly produced (which is not the same as being produced anew again and again). It is precisely the possibility of a repetition which does not consolidate that dissociated unity, the subject, but which proliferates effects which undermine the force of normalization. The term which not only names, but forms and frames the subject—let us use Foucault's example of homosexuality—mobilizes a reverse discourse against the very regime of normalization by which it is spawned. This is, of course, not a pure opposition, for the same "homosexuality" will be deployed first in the service of normalizing heterosexuality and second in the service of its own depathologization. This term will carry the risk of the former meaning in the latter, but it would be a mistake to think that simply by speaking the term one either transcends heterosexual normalization or becomes its instrument.

The risk of renormalization is persistently there: consider the one who in defiant "outness" declares his/her homosexuality only to receive the response, "Ah yes, so you are that, and only that." Whatever you say will be read back as an overt or subtle manifestation of your essential homosexuality. (One should not underestimate how exhausting it is to be expected to be an "out" homosexual all the time, whether the expectation comes from gay and lesbian allies or their foes.) Here Foucault cites and reworks the possibility of resignification, of mobilizing politically what Nietzsche, in *On the Genealogy of Morals*, called the "sign chain." There Nietzsche argues that the uses to which a given sign is originally put are "worlds apart" from the uses to which it then becomes available. This temporal gap between usages produces the possibility of a reversal of signification, but also opens the way for an inauguration of signifying possibilities that exceed those to which the term has been previously bound.

The Foucaultian subject is never fully constituted in subjection, then; it is repeatedly constituted in subjection, and it is in the possibility of a repetition that repeats against its origin that subjection might be understood to draw its inadvertently enabling power. From a psychoanalytic perspective, however, we might ask whether this possibility of resistance to a constituting or subjectivating power can be derived from what is "in" or "of" discourse. What can we make of the way in which discourses not only constitute the domains of the speakable, but are themselves bounded through the production of a constitutive outside: the unspeakable, the unsignifiable?

From a Lacanian perspective, one might well question whether the effects of the psyche can be said to be exhausted in what can be signified or whether there is not, over and against this signifying body, a domain of the psyche which contests legibility. If, according to psychoanalysis, the subject is not the same as the psyche from which it emerges and if, for Foucault, the subject is not the same as the body from which it emerges, then perhaps the body has come to substitute for the psyche in Foucault—that is, as that which exceeds and confounds the injunctions of normalization. Is this a body pure and simple, or does "the body" come to stand for a certain operation of the psyche, one which is distinctly different, if not directly opposed to, the soul figured as an imprisoning effect? Perhaps Foucault himself has invested the body with a psychic meaning that he cannot elaborate within the terms that he uses. How does the process of subjectivation, the disciplinary production of the subject, break down, if it does, in both Foucaultian and psychoanalytic theory? Whence does that failure emerge, and what are its consequences?

Consider the Althusserian notion of interpellation, in which a subject is constituted by being hailed, addressed, named.[15] For the most part, it seems, Althusser believed that this social demand—one might call it a symbolic injunction—actually produced the kinds of subjects it named. He gives the example of the policeman on the street yelling "Hey you there!," and concludes that this call importantly constitutes the one it addresses and sites. The scene is clearly a disciplinary one; the policeman's call is an effort to bring someone back in line. Yet we might also understand it in Lacanian terms as the call of symbolic constitution. As Althusser himself insists, this performative effort of naming can only *attempt* to bring its addressee into being: there is always the risk of a certain *misrecognition*. If one misrecognizes that effort to produce the subject, the production itself falters. The one who is hailed may fail to hear, misread the call, turn the other way, answer to another name, insist on not being addressed in that way. Indeed, the domain of the imaginary is demarcated by Althusser as precisely the domain that makes *misrecognition* possible. The name is called, and I am sure it is my name, but it isn't. The name is called, and I am sure that a name is being called, my name, but it is in someone's incomprehensible speech, or worse, it is someone coughing, or worse, a radiator which for a moment approximates a human voice. Or I am sure that no one has noticed my transgression, and that it is not my name that is being called, but only a coughing passerby, the high pitch of the heating mechanism—but it is my name, and yet I do not recognize myself in the subject that the name, at this moment, installs.[16]

Consider the force of this dynamic of interpellation and misrecognition when the name is not a proper name but a social category,[17] and hence a signifier capable of being interpreted in a number of divergent and conflictual ways. To be hailed as a "woman" or "Jew" or "queer" or "Black" or "Chicana" may be heard or interpreted as an affirmation or an insult, depending on the context in which the hailing occurs (where context is the effective historicity and spatiality of the sign). If that name is called, there is more often than not some hesitation about whether or how to respond, for what is at stake is whether the temporary totalization performed by the name is politically enabling or paralyzing, whether the foreclosure, indeed the violence, of the totalizing reduction of identity performed by that particular hailing is politically strategic or regressive or, if paralyzing and regressive, also enabling in some way.

The Althusserian use of Lacan centers on the function of the imaginary as the permanent possibility of *misrecognition*, that is, the incommensurability between symbolic demand (the name that is interpellated) and the instability and unpredictability of its appropriation. If the interpellated name seeks to accomplish the identity to which it refers, it begins as a performative process which is nevertheless derailed in the imaginary, for the imaginary is surely preoccupied with the law, structured by the law, but does not immediately obey the law. For the Lacanian, then, the imaginary signifies the impossibility of the discursive—that is, symbolic—constitution of identity. Identity can never be fully totalized by the symbolic, for what it fails to order will emerge within the imaginary as a disorder, a site where identity is contested.

Hence, in a Lacanian vein, Jacqueline Rose formulates the unconscious as that which thwarts any effort of the symbolic to constitute sexed identity coherently and fully, an unconscious indicated by the slips and gaps that characterize the workings of the imaginary in language. I quote a passage which has benefitted many of us who have sought to find in psychoanalysis a principle of resistance to given forms of social reality:

> The unconscious constantly reveals the "failure" of identity. Because there is no continuity of psychic life, so there is no stability of sexual identity, no position for women (or for men) which is ever simply achieved. Nor does psychoanalysis see such "failure" as a special-case inability or an individual deviancy from the norm. "Failure" is not a moment to be regretted in a process of adaptation, or development into normality, . . . "failure" is something endlessly repeated and relived moment by moment throughout our individual histories. It appears not only in the symptom, but also in dreams, in slips of the tongue and in forms of sexual pleasure which are pushed to the sidelines of the norm. . . . there is a resistance to identity at the very heart of psychic life.[18]

In *Discipline and Punish*, Foucault presumes the efficacy of the symbolic demand, its performative capacity to constitute the subject whom it names. In *The History of Sexuality, Volume 1*, however, there is both a rejection of "a single locus of Revolt"—which would presumably include the psyche, the imaginary, or the unconscious within its purview—and an affirmation of multiple possibilities of resistance enabled by power itself. For Foucault, resistance cannot be *outside* the law in another register (the imaginary) or in that which eludes the constitutive power of the law.

there is no single locus of great Refusal, no soul of revolt, source of all rebellions, or pure law of the revolutionary. Instead there is a plurality of resistances, each of them a special case: resistances that are possible, necessary, improbable; others that are spontaneous, savage, solitary, concerted, rampant, or violent; still others that are quick to compromise, interested, or sacrificial; by definition, they can only exist in the strategic field of power relations. But this does not mean that they are only a reaction or rebound, forming with respect to the basic domination an underside that is in the end always passive, doomed to perpetual defeat.[19]

This last caricature of power, although clearly written with Marcuse in mind, recalls the effect of the Lacanian law, which produces its own "failure" at the level of the psyche, but which can never be displaced or reformulated by that psychic resistance. The imaginary thwarts the efficacy of the symbolic law but cannot turn back upon the law, demanding or effecting its reformulation. In this sense, psychic resistance thwarts the law in its effects, but cannot redirect the law or its effects. Resistance is thus located in a domain that is virtually powerless to alter the law that it opposes. Hence, psychic resistance presumes the continuation of the law in its anterior, symbolic form and, in that sense, contributes to its status quo. In such a view, resistance appears doomed to perpetual defeat.

In contrast, Foucault formulates resistance as an effect of the very power that it is said to oppose. This insistence on the dual possibility of being both *constituted* by the law and *an effect of resistance* to the law marks a departure from the Lacanian framework, for where Lacan restricts the notion of social power to the symbolic domain and delegates resistance to the imaginary, Foucault recasts the symbolic as relations of power and understands resistance as an effect of power. Foucault's conception initiates a shift from a discourse on law, conceived as juridical (and presupposing a subject subordinated by power), to a discourse on power, which is a field of productive, regulatory, and contestatory relations. For Foucault, the symbolic produces the possibility of its own subversions, and these subversions are unanticipated effects of symbolic interpellations.

The notion of "the symbolic" does not address the multiplicity of power vectors upon which Foucault insists, for power in Foucault not only consists in the reiterated elaboration of norms or interpellating demands, but is formative or productive, malleable, multiple, proliferative, and conflictual. Moreover, in its resignifications, the law itself is transmuted into that which opposes and exceeds its original purposes. In this sense, disciplinary discourse does not unilaterally constitute a subject in Foucault, or rather, if it does, it *simultaneously* constitutes the condition for the subject's de-constitution. What is brought into being through the performative effect of the interpellating demand is much more than a "subject," for the "subject" created is not for that reason fixed in place: it becomes the occasion for a further making. Indeed, I would add, a subject only remains a subject through a reiteration or rearticulation of itself as a subject, and this dependency of the subject on repetition for coherence may constitute that subject's incoherence, its incomplete character. This repetition or, better, iterability thus becomes the non-place of subversion, the possibility of a re-embodying of the subjectivating norm that can redirect its normativity.

Consider the inversions of "woman" and "woman," depending on the staging and address of their performance, of "queer" and "queer," depending on pathologizing or contestatory modes. Both examples concern, not an opposition between reactionary and progressive usage, but rather a progressive usage that requires and repeats the reactionary in order to effect a subversive reterritorialization. For Foucault, then, the disciplinary apparatus produces subjects, but as a consequence of that production, it brings into discourse the conditions for subverting that apparatus itself. In other words, the law turns against itself and spawns versions of itself which oppose and proliferate its animating purposes. The strategic question for Foucault is, then, how can we work the power relations by which we are worked, and in what direction?

In his later interviews, Foucault suggests that identities are formed within contemporary political arrangements in relation to certain requirements of the liberal state, ones which presume that the assertion of rights and claims to entitlement can only be made on the basis of a singular and injured identity. The more specific identities become, the more totalized an identity becomes by that very specificity. Indeed, we might understand this contemporary phenomenon as the movement by which a juridical apparatus produces the field of possible political subjects. Because for Foucault the disciplinary apparatus of the state operates through the totalizing production of individuals, and because this totalization of the individual extends the jurisdiction of the state (i.e., by transforming individuals into subjects of the state), Foucault will call for a remaking of subjectivity beyond the shackles of the juridical law. In this sense, what we call identity politics is produced by a state which can only allocate recognition and rights to subjects totalized by the particularity that constitutes their plaintiff status. In calling for an overthrow, as it were, of such an arrangement, Foucault is not calling for the release of a hidden or repressed subjectivity, but rather, for a radical making of subjectivity formed in and against the historical hegemony of the juridical subject:

Maybe the target nowadays is not to discover what we are, but to refuse what we are. We have to imagine and build up what we could be to get rid of this kind of political "double bind," which is the simultaneous individualization and totalization of modern power structures. . . . The conclusion would be that the political, ethical, social, philosophical problem of our days is not to try to liberate us both from the state, and from the state's institutions, but to liberate us from the state and the type of individualization which is linked to the state. We have to promote new forms of subjectivity through the refusal of this kind of individuality which has been imposed on us for several centuries.[20]

Two sets of questions emerge from the above analysis. First, why can Foucault formulate resistance in relation to the disciplinary power of sexuality in *The History of Sexuality*, whereas in *Discipline and Punish* disciplinary power appears to determine docile bodies incapable of resistance? Is there something about the relationship of *sexuality* to power that conditions the possibility of resistance in the first text, and a noted absence of a consideration of sexuality from the discussion of power and bodies in the second? Note that in the *History of Sexuality* the repressive function of the law is undermined precisely through becoming itself the object of erotic investment and excitation. Disciplinary apparatus fails to repress sexuality precisely because the apparatus is itself eroticized, becoming the occasion for the *incitement of sexuality* and, therefore, undoing its own repressive aims.

Second, with this transferable property of sexual investments in mind, we might ask what conditions the possibility Foucault invites, that of refusing the type of individuality correlated with the disciplinary apparatus of the modern state?

And how do we account for *attachment* to precisely the kind of state-linked individuality that reconsolidates the juridical law? To what extent has the disciplinary apparatus that attempts to produce and totalize identity become an abiding object of passionate attachment? We cannot simply throw off the identities we have become, and Foucault's call to "refuse" those identities will certainly be met with resistance. If we reject theoretically the source of resistance in a psychic domain that is said to precede or exceed the social,[21] as we must, can we reformulate psychic resistance *in terms of the social* without that reformulation becoming a domestication or normalization? (Must the social always be equated with the given and the normalizable?) In particular, how are we to understand, not merely the disciplinary production of the subject, but the disciplinary cultivation of *an attachment to subjection*?

Such a postulation may raise the question of masochism—indeed, the question of masochism in subject-formation—yet it does not answer the question of the status of "attachment" or "investment." Here emerges the grammatical problem by which an attachment appears to precede the subject who might be said to "have" it. Yet it seems crucial to suspend the usual grammatical requirements and consider an inversion of terms such that certain attachments precede and condition the formation of subjects (the visualization of libido in the mirror stage, the sustaining of that projected image through time as the discursive function of the name). Is this then an ontology of libido or investment that is in some sense prior to and separable from a subject, or is every such investment from the start bound up with a reflexivity that is stabilized (within the imaginary) as the ego? If the ego is composed of identifications, and identification is the resolution of desire, then the ego is the residue of desire, the effect of incorporations which, Freud argues in *The Ego and the Id*, trace a lineage of attachment and loss.

In Freud's view, the formation of conscience enacts an attachment to prohibition which founds the subject in its reflexivity. Under the pressure of the ethical law, a subject emerges who is capable of reflexivity, that is, who takes him/herself as an object, and so mistakes him/herself, since he/she is, by virtue of that founding prohibition, at an infinite distance from his/her origin. Only on the condition of a separation enforced through prohibition does a subject emerge, formed through the attachment to prohibition (in obedience to it, but also eroticizing it). And this prohibition is all the more savory precisely because it is bound up in the narcissistic circuit that wards off the dissolution of the subject into psychosis.[22]

For Foucault, a subject is formed and then invested with a sexuality by a regime of power. If the very process of subject-formation, however, requires a preemption of sexuality, a founding prohibition that prohibits a certain desire but itself becomes a focus of desire, then a subject is formed through the prohibition of a sexuality, a prohibition that at the same time forms this sexuality—and the subject who is said to bear it. This view disputes the Foucaultian notion that psychoanalysis presumes the exteriority of the law to desire, for it maintains that there is no desire without the law that forms and sustains the very desire it prohibits. Indeed, prohibition becomes an odd form of preservation, a way of eroticizing the law that would abolish eroticism, but which only works by compelling eroticization. In this sense, a "sexual identity" is a productive contradiction in terms, for identity is formed through a prohibition on some dimension of the very sexuality it is said to bear, and sexuality, when it is tied to identity, is always in some sense undercutting itself.

This is not necessarily a static contradiction, for the signifiers of identity are not structurally determined in advance. If Foucault could argue that a sign could be taken up, used for purposes counter to those for which it was designed, then he understood that even the most noxious terms could be owned, that the most injurious interpellations could also be the site of radical reoccupation and resignification. But what lets us occupy the discursive site of injury? How are we animated and mobilized by that discursive site and its injury, such that our very attachment to it becomes the condition for our resignification of it? Called by an injurious name, I come into social being, and because I have a certain inevitable attachment to my existence, because a certain narcissism takes hold of any term that confers existence, I am led to embrace the terms that injure me because they constitute me socially. The self-colonizing trajectory of certain forms of identity politics are symptomatic of this paradoxical embrace of the injurious term. As a further paradox, then, only by occupying—being occupied by—that injurious term can I resist and oppose it, recasting the power that constitutes me as the power I oppose. In this way, a certain place for psychoanalysis is secured in that any mobilization against subjection will take subjection as its resource, and that attachment to an injurious interpellation will, by way of a necessarily alienated narcissism, become the condition under which resignifying that interpellation becomes possible. This will not be an unconscious outside of power, but rather something like the unconscious of power itself, in its traumatic and productive iterability.

If, then, we understand certain kinds of interpellations to confer identity, those injurious interpellations will constitute identity through injury. This is not the same as saying that such an identity will remain always and forever rooted in its injury as long as it remains an identity, but it does imply that the possibilities of resignification will rework and unsettle the passionate attachment to subjection without which subject formation—and re-formation—cannot succeed.

"Conscience Doth Make Subjects of Us All"

Althusser's Subjection

Althusser's doctrine of interpellation continues to structure contemporary debate on subject formation, offering a way to account for a subject who comes into being as a consequence of language, yet always within its terms. The theory of interpellation appears to stage a social scene in which a subject is hailed, the subject turns around, and the subject then accepts the terms by which he or she is hailed. This is, no doubt, a scene both punitive and reduced, for the call is made by an officer of "the Law," and this officer is cast as singular and speaking. Clearly we might object that the "call" arrives severally and in implicit and unspoken ways, that the scene is never quite as dyadic as Althusser claims, but these objections have been rehearsed, and "interpellation" as a doctrine continues to survive its critique. If we accept that the scene is exemplary and allegorical, then it never needs to happen for its effectivity to be presumed. Indeed, if it is allegorical in Benjamin's sense, then the process literalized by the allegory is precisely what resists narration, what exceeds the narrativizability of events.[1] Interpellation, on this account, is not an event, but a certain way of *staging the call*, where the call, as staged, becomes deliteralized in the course of its exposition or *darstellung*. The call itself is also figured as a demand to align oneself with the law, a turning around (to face the law, to find a face for the law?), and an entrance into the language of self-ascription—"Here I am"—through the appropriation of guilt.

Why does subject formation appear to take place only upon the acceptance of guilt, so that there is no "I" who might ascribe a place to itself, who might be announced in speech, without first a self-attribution of guilt, a submission to the law through an acceptance of its demand for conformity? The one who turns around in response to the call does not respond to a demand to turn around. The turning around is an act that is, as it were, conditioned both by the "voice" of the law and by the responsiveness of the one hailed by the law. The "turning around" is a strange sort of middle ground (taking place, perhaps, in a strange sort of "middle voice"),[2] which is determined both by the law and the addressee, but by neither unilaterally or exhaustively. Although there would be no turning around without first having been hailed, neither would there be a turning around without some readiness to turn. But where and when does the calling of the name solicit the turning around, the anticipatory move toward identity? How and why does the subject turn, anticipating the conferral of identity through the self-ascription of guilt? What kind of relation already binds these two such that the subject knows to turn, knows that something is to be gained from such a turn? How might we think of this "turn" as prior to subject formation, a prior complicity with the law without which no subject emerges? The turn toward the law is thus a turn against oneself, a turning back on oneself that constitutes the movement of conscience. But how does the reflex of conscience paralyze the critical interrogation of the law at the same time that it figures the subject's uncritical relation to the law as a condition of subjectivation? The one addressed is compelled to turn toward the law prior to any possibility of asking a set of critical questions: Who is speaking? Why should I turn around? Why should I accept the terms by which I am hailed?

This means that prior to any possibility of a critical understanding of the law is an openness or vulnerability to the law, exemplified in the turn toward the law, in the anticipation of culling an identity through identifying with the one who has broken the law. Indeed, the law is broken prior to any possibility of having access to the law, and so "guilt" is prior to knowledge of the law and is, in this sense, always strangely innocent. The possibility of a critical view of the law is thus limited by what might be understood as a prior desire for the law, a passionate complicity with law, without which no subject can exist. For the "I" to launch its critique, it must first understand that the "I" itself is dependent upon its complicitous desire for the law to make possible its own existence. A critical review of the law will not, therefore, undo the force of conscience unless the one who offers that critique is willing, as it were, to be undone by the critique that he or she performs.

It is important to remember that the turn toward the law is not necessitated by the hailing; it is compelling, in a less than logical sense, because it promises identity. If the law speaks in the name of a self-identical subject (Althusser cites the utterance of the Hebrew God: "I am that I am"), how is it that conscience might deliver or restore a self to oneness with itself, to the postulation of self-identity that becomes the precondition of the linguistic consolidation "Here I am"?

Yet how might we site the vulnerability of subjectivation precisely in that turn (toward the law, against the self), which precedes and anticipates the acceptance of guilt, a turn that eludes subjectivation even as it conditions it? How does this "turn" figure a conscience that might be rendered less conscientious than Althusser would render it? And how does Althusser's sanctification of the scene of interpellation make the possibility of becoming a "bad" subject more remote and less incendiary than it might well be?

The doctrine of interpellation appears to presuppose a prior and unelaborated doctrine of conscience, a turning back upon oneself in the sense that Nietzsche described in *On the Genealogy of Morals*.[3] This readiness to accept guilt to gain a purchase on identity is linked to a highly religious scenario of a nominating call that comes from God and that constitutes the subject by appealing to a need for the law, an original guilt that the law promises to assuage through the conferral of identity. How does this religious figuration of interpellation restrain in advance any possibility of critical intervention in the workings of the law, any undoing of the subject without which the law cannot proceed?

The mention of conscience in Althusser's "Ideology and Ideological State Apparatuses"[4] has received little critical attention, even though the term, taken together with the example of religious authority to illustrate the force of ideology, suggests that the theory of ideology is supported by a complicated set of theological metaphors. Although Althusser explicitly introduces "the Church" merely as an *example* of ideological interpellation, it appears that ideology in his terms cannot be thought except through the metaphorics of religious authority. The final section of "Ideology" is entitled "An Example: The Christian Religious Ideology" and makes explicit the exemplary status that religious institutions have occupied in the preceding section of the essay. Those examples include:

the putative "eternity" of ideology; the explicit analogy between the "obviousness of ideology" and St. Paul's notion of the "Logos" in which we are said to "live, move and have our being"; Pascal's prayer as an instance of ritual in which assuming the posture of kneeling gives rise over time to belief; belief itself as the institutionally reproduced condition of ideology; and the deifying capitalization of "Family," "Church," "School," and "State."

Although the last section of the essay seeks to explicate and expose the example of religious authority, this exposure lacks the power to defuse the force of ideology. Althusser's own writing, he concedes, invariably enacts what it thematizes,[5] and thus promises no enlightened escape from ideology through this articulation. To illustrate the power of ideology to constitute subjects, Althusser has recourse to the example of the divine voice that names, and in naming, brings its subjects into being. In claiming that social ideology operates in an analogous way, Althusser inadvertently assimilates social interpellation to the divine performative. The example of ideology thus assumes the status of a paradigm for thinking ideology as such, whereby the inevitable structures of ideology are established textually through religious metaphor: the authority of the "voice" of ideology, the "voice" of interpellation, is figured as a voice almost impossible to refuse. The force of interpellation in Althusser is derived from the examples by which it is ostensibly illustrated, most notably, God's voice in the naming of Peter (and Moses) and its secularization in the postulated voice of the representative of state authority: the policeman's voice in the hailing of the wayward pedestrian with "Hey you there!"

In other words, the divine power of naming structures the theory of interpellation that accounts for the ideological constitution of the subject. Baptism exemplifies the linguistic means by which the subject is compelled into social being. God names "Peter," and this address establishes God as the origin of Peter;[6] the name remains attached to Peter permanently by virtue of the implied and continuous presence in the name of the one who names him. Within the terms of Althusser's examples, however, this naming cannot be accomplished without a certain readiness or anticipatory desire on the part of the one addressed. To the extent that the naming is an address, there is an addressee prior to the address; but given that the address is a name which creates what it names, there appears to be no "Peter" without the name "Peter."

Indeed, "Peter" does not exist without the name that supplies the linguistic guarantee of existence. In this sense, as a prior and essential condition of the formation of the subject, there is a certain readiness to be compelled by the authoritative interpellation, a readiness which suggests that one is, as it were, already in relation to the voice before the response, already implicated in the terms of the animating misrecognition by an authority to which one subsequently yields. Or perhaps one has already yielded before one turns around, and that turning is merely a sign of an inevitable submission by which one is established as a subject positioned in language as a possible addressee. In this sense, the scene with the police is a belated and redoubled scene, one which renders explicit a founding submission for which no such scene would prove adequate. If that submission brings the subject into being, then the narrative that seeks to tell the story of that submission can proceed only by exploiting grammar for its fictional effects. The narrative that seeks to account for how the subject comes into being presumes the grammatical "subject" prior to the account of its genesis. Yet the founding submission that has not yet resolved into the subject would be precisely the non-narrativizable prehistory of the subject, a paradox which calls the very narrative of subject formation into question. If there is no subject except as a consequence of this subjection, the narrative that would explain this requires that the temporality not be true, for the grammar of that narrative presupposes that there is no subjection without a subject who undergoes it.

Is this founding submission a kind of yielding prior to any question of psychological motivation? How are we to understand the psychic disposition at work at the moment in which the pedestrian responds to the law? What conditions and informs that response? Why would the person on the street respond to "Hey you there!" by turning around? What is the significance of turning to face a voice that calls from behind? This turning toward the voice of the law is a sign of a certain desire to be beheld by and perhaps also to behold the face of authority, a visual rendering of an auditory scene—a mirror stage or, perhaps more appropriately, an "acoustic mirror"[7]—that permits the misrecognition without which the sociality of the subject cannot be achieved. This subjectivation is, according to Althusser, a *mis*recognition, a false and provisional totalization; what precipitates this desire for the law, this lure of misrecognition offered in the reprimand that establishes subordination as the price of subjectivation? This account appears to imply that social existence, existence as a subject, can be purchased only through a guilty embrace of the law, where guilt guarantees the intervention of the law and, hence, the continuation of the subject's existence. If the subject can only assure his/her existence in terms of the law, and the law requires subjection for subjectivation, then, perversely, one may (always already) yield to the law in order to continue to assure one's own existence. The yielding to the law might then be read as the compelled consequence of a narcissistic attachment to one's continuing existence.

Althusser takes up guilt explicitly in the narrative, however reliable, of his murder of Hélène, his wife, in which he narrates, in a telling reversal of the police scene in "Ideology," how he rushed into the street calling for the police in order to deliver himself up to the law.[8] This calling for the police is a peculiar inversion of hailing which "Ideology" presupposes without explicitly thematizing. Without exploiting the biographical, I want to pursue the theoretical importance of this reversal of the scene with the police, in which the man on the street calls for the police rather than responding to the police's call. In "Ideology," guilt and conscience operate implicitly in relation to an ideological demand, an animating reprimand, in the account of subject formation. The present chapter attempts to reread that essay to understand how interpellation is essentially figured through the religious example. The exemplary status of religious authority underscores the paradox of how the very possibility of subject formation depends upon a passionate pursuit of a recognition which, within the terms of the religious example, is inseparable from a condemnation.

Another way of posing this question would be to ask: How is Althusser's text implicated in the "conscience" that it seeks to explain? To what extent is the persistence of the theological model a symptom, one that compels a symptomatic reading? In his introductory essay to *Reading Capital*, Althusser suggests that every text must be read for the "invisible" that appears within the world that theory renders visible.[9] In a recent consideration of Althusser's notion of "symptomatic reading," Jean-Marie Vincent remarks that "a text is not interesting only because it is organized logically, because of the apparently rigorous way in which it develops its arguments, but also because of what disorganizes its order, because of all that weakens it."[10] Neither Althusser nor Vincent considers the possibility that the exemplary status of certain metaphors may occasion a symptomatic reading that "weakens" rigorous argument. Yet in Althusser's own text, reconsidering the central religious tropes of the voice of the law and conscience enables one to question what has become, within recent literary studies, an unnecessary tension between the reading of metaphor and the reading of ideology. To the extent that Althusser's religious analogies are understood as merely illustrative, they are set apart from the rigorous argumentation of the text itself, offered in pedagogical paraphrasis. Yet the performative force of the voice of religious authority becomes exemplary for the theory of interpellation, thus extending through example the putative force of divine naming to the social authorities by which the subject is hailed into social being. I do not mean to suggest that the "truth" of Althusser's text can be discovered in how the figural disrupts "rigorous" conceptualization. Such an approach romanticizes the figural as essentially disruptive, whereas figures may well compound and intensify conceptual claims. The concern here has a more specific textual aim, namely, to show how figures—examples and analogies—inform and extend conceptualizations, implicating the text in an ideological sanctification of religious authority which it can expose only by reenacting that authority.

For Althusser, the efficacy of ideology consists in part in the formation of *conscience*, where the notion "conscience" is understood to place restrictions on what is speakable or, more generally, representable. Conscience cannot be conceptualized as a self-restriction, if that relation is construed as a pregiven reflexivity, a turning back upon itself performed by a ready-made subject. Instead, it designates a kind of turning back—

a reflexivity—which constitutes the condition of possibility for the subject to form. Reflexivity is constituted through this moment of conscience, this turning back upon oneself, which is simultaneous with a turning toward the law. This self-restriction does not internalize an external law: the model of internalization takes for granted that an "internal" and "external" have already been formed. Instead, this self-restriction is prior to the subject. It constitutes the inaugurating reflexive turn of the subject, enacted in anticipation of the law and hence determined by, having prejudicative foreknowledge of, the law. Conscience is fundamental to the production and regulation of the citizen-subject, for conscience turns the individual around, makes him/her available to the subjectivating reprimand. The law redoubles that reprimand, however: the turning back is a turning toward. How are these turns to be thought together, without reducing one to the other?

Before the police or the church authorities arrive on the Althusserian scene, there is a reference to prohibition which, in a Lacanian vein, is linked with the very possibility of speech. Althusser links the emergence of a consciousness—and a conscience ("la conscience civique et professionelle")—with the problem of speaking properly (*bien parler*).[11] "Speaking properly" appears to be an instance of the ideological work of acquiring skills, a process central to the formation of the subject. The "diverse skills" of labor power must be reproduced, and increasingly this reproduction happens "outside the firm" and *in school*, that is, outside production and in educational institutions. The skills to be learned are, above all, *the skills of speech*. The first mention of "conscience," which will turn out to be central to the success or efficacy of interpellation, is linked to the acquisition of mastery, to learning how to "speak properly." The reproduction of the subject takes place through the reproduction of linguistic skills, constituting, as it were, the rules and attitudes observed "by every agent in the division of labour." In this sense the rules of proper speech are also the rules by which *respect* is proferred or withheld. Workers are taught to *speak* properly and managers learn to speak to workers "in the right way [*bien commander*]" (131–32/72).

Language skills are said to be mastered and masterable, yet this mastery is figured by Althusser quite clearly as a kind of submission: "the reproduction of labor power requires not only a reproduction of (the laborer's) skills, but also, at the same time, a reproduction of its submission to the rules of the established order [*soumission à l'idéologie dominante*]" (132/72). This submission to the rules of the dominant ideology leads in the next paragraph to the problematic of *subjection*, which carries the double meaning of having submitted to these rules and becoming constituted within sociality by virtue of this submission.

Althusser writes that "the school . . . teaches 'know-how' [skills; *des 'savoir-faire'*] . . . in forms which ensure *subjection to the ruling ideology* [l'assujetissement à l'idéologie dominante] or [*ou*] the mastery of its 'practice'" (133/73). Consider the logical effect of the disjunctive "or" in the middle of this formulation: "subjection *to* the ruling ideology or"—put in different, yet equivalent terms—"the mastery *of* its 'practice'" (my emphasis). The more a practice is mastered, the more fully subjection is achieved. Submission and mastery take place simultaneously, and this paradoxical simultaneity constitutes the ambivalence of subjection. Though one might expect submission to consist in yielding to an externally imposed dominant order and to be marked by a loss of control and mastery, paradoxically, it is itself marked by mastery. The binary frame of mastery/submission is forfeited by Althusser as he recasts submission precisely and paradoxically as a kind of mastery. In this view, neither submission nor mastery is *performed by a subject*; the lived simultaneity of submission as mastery, and mastery as submission, is the condition of possibility for the emergence of the subject.

The conceptual problem here is underscored by a grammatical one in which there can be no subject prior to a submission, and yet there is a grammatically induced "need to know" *who* undergoes this submission in order to become a subject. Althusser introduces the term "individual" as a place-holder to satisfy provisionally this grammatical need, but what might ultimately fit the grammatical requirement will not be a static grammatical subject. The grammar of the subject emerges only as a consequence of the process we are trying to describe. Because we are, as it were, trapped within the grammatical time of the subject (e.g., "we are trying to describe," "we are trapped"), it is almost impossible to ask after the genealogy of its construction without presupposing that construction in asking the question.

What, prior to the subject, accounts for its formation? Althusser begins "Ideology and Ideological State Apparatuses" by referring to the reproduction of social relations, specified as the reproduction of social skills. He then distinguishes between skills reproduced in the firm and those reproduced in education. The subject is formed with respect to the latter. In a sense, this reproduction of relations is prior to the subject who is formed in its course. Yet the two cannot, strictly speaking, be thought without each other.

The reproduction of social relations, the reproduction of skills, is the reproduction of subjection. But the reproduction of labor is not central here—the central reproduction is one proper to the subject and takes place in relation to language and to the formation of conscience. For Althusser, to perform tasks "conscientiously" is to perform them, as it were, again and again, to reproduce those skills and, in reproducing them, to acquire mastery. Althusser places "conscientiously" in quotation marks ("pour s'acquitter 'consciencieusement' de leur tâche," 73), thus bringing into relief the way in which labor is moralized. The moral sense of *s'acquitter* is lost in its translation as "to perform": if the mastery of a set of skills is to be construed as *an acquitting of oneself*, then this mastery of *savoir-faire* defends one against an accusation; quite literally, it is the accused's declaration of innocence. To acquit oneself "conscientiously" is, then, to construe labor as a confession of innocence, a display or proof of guiltlessness in the face of the demand for confession implied by an insistent accusation.

"Submission" to the rules of the dominant ideology might then be understood as a submission to the necessity to prove innocence in the face of accusation, a submission to the demand for proof, an execution of that proof, and acquisition of the status of the subject in and through compliance with the terms of the interrogative law. To become a "subject" is thus to have been presumed guilty, then tried and declared innocent. Because this declaration is not a single act but a status incessantly *reproduced*, to become a "subject" is to be continuously in the process of acquitting oneself of the accusation of guilt. It is to have become an emblem of lawfulness, a citizen in good standing, but one for whom that status is tenuous, indeed, one who has known—somehow, somewhere—what it is *not* to have that standing and hence to have been cast out as guilty. Yet because this guilt conditions the subject, it constitutes the prehistory of the subjection to the law by which the subject is produced. Here one might usefully conjecture that the reason there are so few references to "bad subjects" in Althusser is that the term tends toward the oxymoronic. To be "bad" is not yet to be a subject, not yet to have acquitted oneself of the allegation of guilt.[12]

This performance is not simply *in accord* with these skills, for there is no subject prior to their performing; performing skills laboriously works the subject into its status as a social being. There is guilt, and then a repetitive practice by which skills are acquired, and then and only then an assumption of the grammatical place within the social as a subject.

To say that the subject performs according to a set of skills is, as it were, to take grammar at its word: there is a subject who encounters a set of skills to be learned, learns them or fails to learn them, and then and only then can it be said either to have mastered those skills or not. To master a set of skills is not simply to accept a set of skills, but to reproduce them in and as one's own activity. This is not simply to act according to a set of rules, but to embody rules in the course of action and to reproduce those rules in embodied rituals of action.[13]

What leads to this reproduction? Clearly, it is not merely a mechanistic appropriation of norms, nor is it a voluntaristic appropriation. It is neither simple behaviorism nor a deliberate project. To the extent that it precedes the formation of the subject, it is not yet of the order of consciousness, and yet this involuntary compulsion is not a mechanistically induced effect. The notion of ritual suggests that it is performed, and that in the repetition of performance a belief is spawned, which is then incorporated into the performance in its subsequent operations. But inherent to any performance is a compulsion to "acquit oneself," and so prior to any performance is an anxiety and a knowingness which becomes articulate and animating only on the occasion of the reprimand.

Is it possible to separate the psychic dimension of this ritu-alistic repetition from the "acts" by which it is animated and reanimated? The very notion of ritual is meant to render be-lief and practice inseparable. Yet the Slovenian critic Mladen Dolar argues that Althusser fails to account for the psyche as a separate dimension. Dolar counsels a return to Lacan, much in the same way that Slavoj Žižek suggests a necessary com-plementarity between Althusser and Lacan.[14] To insist on the separability of the psyche from social practice is to intensify the religious metaphorics in Althusser, that is, to figure the psyche as pure ideality, not unlike the ideality of the soul. I turn, then, to Dolar's reading of Althusser in order to consider the tension between the putative ideality of subjectivity and the claim that ideology, including psychic reality, is part of the expanded domain of materiality in the Althusserian sense.

Mladen Dolar's essay "Beyond Interpellation"[15] suggests that Althusser, despite his occasional use of Lacan's theory of the imaginary, fails to appreciate the disruptive potential of psychoanalysis, in particular, the notion of the Real as desig-nating that which never becomes available to subjectivation. Dolar writes, "To put it the simplest way, there is a part of the individual that cannot successfully pass into the subject, an element of 'pre-ideological' and 'presubjective' *materia prima* that comes to haunt subjectivity once it is constituted as such" (75). The use of *"materia prima"* here is significant, for with this phrase Dolar explicitly contests the social account of ma-teriality that Althusser provides. In fact, this *"materia prima"* never *materializes* in the Althusserian sense, never emerges as a practice, a ritual, or a social relation; from the point of view of the social, the "materia prima" is radically *immaterial*. Dolar thus criticizes Althusser for eliding the dimension of subjec-tivity that remains radically immaterial, barred from appearance within materiality. According to Dolar, interpellation can only explain the formation of the subject in a partial way: "for Althusser, the subject is what makes ideology work; for psychoanalysis, the subject emerges where ideology fails. . . . The remainder produced by subjectivation is also invisible from the point of view of interpellation." "Interpellation" he writes, "is a way of avoiding [that remainder]" (76). At stake for Dolar is the need to strengthen the distinction between the domain of the symbolic, understood as communicable speech and social bonds, and that of the psychic, which is ontologically distinct from the social and is defined as the remainder that the notion of the social cannot take into account.

Dolar distinguishes between materiality and interiority, then loosely aligns that distinction with the Althusserian division between the materiality of the state apparatus and the putative ideality of subjectivity. In a formulation with strong Cartesian resonance, Dolar defines subjectivity through the notion of interiority and identifies as material the domain of exteriority (i.e., exterior to the subject). He presupposes that subjectivity consists in both interiority and ideality, whereas materiality belongs to its opposite, the countervailing exterior world.

This manner of distinguishing interior from exterior may well seem strange as a characterization of or extrapolation from Althusser's position. Althusser's distinctive contribution is, after all, to undermine the ontological dualism presupposed by the conventional Marxist distinction between a material base and an ideal or ideological superstructure. He does so by asserting the materiality *of* the ideological: "an ideology always exists in an apparatus, and its practice, or practices. This existence is material." [16]

The constitution of the subject is *material* to the extent that this constitution takes place through *rituals,* and these rituals materialize "the ideas of the subject" (169). What is called "subjectivity," understood as the lived and imaginary experience of the subject, is itself derived from the material rituals by which subjects are constituted. Pascal's believer kneels more than once, necessarily repeating the gesture by which belief is conjured. To understand, more broadly, "the rituals of ideological recognition" (173) by which the subject is constituted is central to the very notion of ideology. But if belief follows from the posture of prayer, if that posture conditions and reiterates belief, then how are we to separate the ideational sphere from the ritual practices by which it is incessantly reinstituted?

Although the question of the subject is not the same as the question of subjectivity, in Dolar's essay it nevertheless remains unclear how those two notions are to be thought together. The notion of "subjectivity" does not have much play in Althusser, except perhaps in the critique of subjectivism, and it is unclear how that term might be transposed onto the terms he uses. This may be Dolar's critical point, namely, that there is not enough of a place for subjectivity in Althusser's text. Dolar's primary critical concern is that Althusser cannot fully take into account the "remainder" produced by subjectivation, the non-phenomenal "kernel of interiority."[17] In fact, Dolar will argue that the distinction between the interior and the exterior is produced through "the introjection of the object" (79). Hence, a primary object is introjected, and that introjection becomes the condition of possibility for the subject. The irrecoverability of that object is, thus, not only the supporting condition of the subject but the persistent threat to its coherence. The Lacanian notion of the Real is cast as the first act of introjection as well as the subject's radical limit.

In Dolar, the ideality of this kernel of interiority sets the limit to both materialization and subjectivation; it constitutes the constitutive lack or the non-symbolizable Real. As foreclosed or introjected, the primary object is lost and idealized at once; the ideality acquired by this object through introjection constitutes the founding ideality of subjectivity. This insight is the one that Althusser appears to miss, and yet Dolar appears to attribute to him the very distinction between materiality and ideality that is insufficiently realized in Althusser's theory:

> there is a step in the emergence of both the subject and the Other that Althusser leaves out and that can perhaps be best illustrated by Althusser's own example. To elucidate the transition between the external materiality of state apparatuses (institutions, practices, rituals, etc.) and the interiority of ideological subjectivity, Althusser borrows a famous suggestion from Pascal, namely his scandalous piece of advice that the best way to become a believer is to follow the religious rituals. (88)

Dolar refers to this as a "senseless ritual," and then reverses the Althusserian account in order to establish that the creed and the ritual are the effects of "a supposition," that ritual follows belief, but is not its condition of production. Dolar underscores the inability of Althusser's theory of ritual practice to account for the motivation to pray: "What made him follow the ritual? Why did he/she consent to repeat a series of senseless gestures?" (89).

Dolar's questions are impossible to satisfy in Althusser's terms, but the very presuppositions of Dolar's questions can be countered with an Althusserian explanation. That Dolar presumes a consenting subject prior to the performance of a ritual suggests that he presumes a volitional subject must already be in place to give an account of motivation. But how does this consenting subject come to be? This supposing and consenting subject appears to precede and condition the "entrance" into the symbolic and, hence, the becoming of a subject. The circularity is clear, but how is it to be understood? Is it a failing of Althusser not to provide the subject prior to the formation of the subject, or does his "failure" indicate only that the grammatical requirements of the narrative work against the account of subject formation that the narrative attempts to provide? To literalize or to ascribe an ontological status to the grammatical requirement of "the subject" is to presume a mimetic relation between grammar and ontology which misses the point, both Althusserian and Lacanian, that the anticipations of grammar are always and only retroactively installed. The grammar that governs the narration of subject formation presumes that the grammatical place for the subject has already been established. In an important sense, then, the grammar that the narrative requires results from the narrative itself. The account of subject formation is thus a double fiction at cross-purposes with itself, repeatedly symptomatizing what resists narration.

Wittgenstein remarks, "We speak, we utter words, and only later get a sense of their life." Anticipation of such sense governs the "empty" ritual that is speech, and ensures its iterability. In this sense, then, we must neither first believe before we kneel nor know the sense of words before we speak. On the contrary, both are performed "on faith" that sense will arrive in and through articulation itself—an anticipation that is not thereby governed by a guarantee of noematic satisfaction. If supposing and consenting are unthinkable outside of the language of supposing and consenting, and this language is itself a sedimentation of ritual forms—the rituals of Cartesianism—then the act by which we might "consent" to kneel is no more and no less ritualistic than the kneeling itself.

Dolar makes his objection explicitly theological by suggesting that Althusser's reformulation of the notion of materiality to include the domain of ideology is too inclusive, that it leaves no room for a non-materializable ideality, the lost and introjected object that inaugurates the formation of the subject. It remains unclear, however, precisely how Dolar reads "materiality" in Althusser, and whether the ritual and hence *temporal* dimension of materiality in Althusser is effaced in favor of a reduction of materiality to the empirically or socially given:

> This is also why Althusser's ardent insistence on materiality is insufficient: the Other that emerges here, the Other of the symbolic order, is not material, and Althusser covers up this non-materiality by talking about the materiality of institutions and practices. If subjectivity can spring up from materially following certain rituals, it is only insofar as those rituals function as a symbolic automatism, that is, insofar as they are governed by an "immaterial" logic supported by the Other. That Other cannot be discovered by scrutinizing materiality . . . what counts is ultimately not that they are material, but that they are ruled by a code and by a repetition. (89)

This last remark formulates an opposition between materiality and repetition that appears to be in direct tension with Althusser's own argumentation. If ideology is material to the extent that it consists in a set of practices, and practices are governed by rituals, then materiality is defined as much by ritual and repetition as it is by more narrowly empiricist conceptions. Moreover, the rituals of ideology are material to the extent that they acquire a *productive* capacity and, in Althusser's text, what rituals produce are subjects.

Dolar explains that rituals produce not subjects, but subjectivity, and can do so only to the extent that they are themselves governed by a symbolic or reiterative logic, a logic which is immaterial. Subjectivity for Dolar is said to "spring up from materially following certain rituals," where the "springing up" is not itself material, but where the notion of "following" a ritual does have a material dimension. Subjectivity arises immaterially from a material ritual performance, but this can happen only on the condition that a logic precedes and supports this ritual performance, an immaterial logic, one which encodes and reenacts the idealizing effects of introjection. But how are we to distinguish the repetition proper to ritual and the repetition proper to the "symbolic automatism"?

Consider the inseparability of those two repetitions in Althusser's description of the materiality of ideas and the ideal in ideology:

> Ideas have disappeared as such (insofar as they are endowed with an ideal or spiritual existence), to the precise extent that it has emerged that their existence is inscribed in the actions of practices governed by rituals defined in the last instance by an ideological apparatus. It therefore appears that the subject acts insofar as he is acted by the following system (set out in the order of its real determination): ideology existing in a material ideological apparatus, prescribing material practices governed by a material ritual, which practices exist in the material actions of a subject acting in all consciousness according to his belief.[18]

Ideas exist "inscribed" in acts that are practices regulated by rituals. Can they appear any other way, and can they have an "existence" outside of ritual? What might it mean to rethink the material not only as regulated repetition, but as a repetition that produces a subject acting in full consciousness according to his belief? The subject's belief is no different from Pascal's; they are both the result of the repetitious conjuring that Althusser calls "materiality."

Dolar argues that Althusser fails to take into account the distinction between materiality and the symbolic, but where would we place "interpellation" on this mapping of the divide? Is it the voice of the symbolic, is it the ritualized voice of the state, or have the two become indissoluble? If, to use Dolar's term, the symbolic acquires its "existence" only in ritual, then what establishes the ideality of that symbolic domain apart from the various modes of its appearance and iterability? Ritual takes place through repetition, and repetition implies the discontinuity of the material, the irreducibility or materiality to phenomenality. The interval by which any repetition takes place does not, strictly speaking, *appear*; it is, as it were, the absence by which the phenomenal is articulated. But this non-appearance or absence is not for that reason an "ideality," for it is bound to the articulation as its constitutive and absent necessity.

Theological resistance to materialism is exemplified in Dolar's explicit defense of Lacan's Cartesian inheritance,[19] his insistance upon the pure ideality of the soul, yet the theological impulse also structures Althusser's work in the figure of the punitive law. Dolar suggests that, though the law successfully regulates its subjects, it cannot touch a certain interior register of love: "there is a remainder involved in the mechanism of interpellation, the left-over of the clean cut, and . . . this remainder can be pinpointed in the experience of love" (85). A bit further on, he asks, "Could one say that love is what we find beyond interpellation?"

Here love is, in Dolar's words, a "forced choice," suggesting that what he expected from the notion of a subject who "consents" to kneel and pray is an account of a "forced consent" of some kind. Love is beyond interpellation precisely because it is understood to be compelled by an immaterial law—the symbolic—over and above the ritualistic laws that govern the various practices of love: "The Other that emerges here, the Other of the symbolic order, is not material, and Althusser covers up this non-materiality by talking about the materiality of institutions and practices" (89). The Other who is lost, introjected, who is said to become the immaterial condition of the subject, inaugurates the repetition specific to the symbolic, the punctuated fantasy of a return that never is or could be completed.

Let us provisionally accept this psychoanalytic account of subject formation, concede that the subject cannot form except through a barred relation to the Other, and even consider this barred Other to reappear as the introjected condition of subject formation, splitting the subject at its inception. Even so, are there other forms of "losing" the Other that are not introjection, and are there various ways of introjecting that Other? Are these terms not culturally elaborated, indeed, ritualized, to such a degree that no meta-scheme of symbolic logic escapes the hermeneutics of social description?

Significantly, though social interpellations are described by Dolar as always "failing" fully to constitute subjects, no such "failure" seems at work in the compulsory character of love. To the extent that primary introjection is an act of love, it is, I would suggest, not an act performed only once, but a re-iterated and indeed ritual affair. But what is to keep us from making the analogy that we fall in love in much the same way we kneel and pray, or that we may well be doing one when we think we are doing the other?

Yet Dolar's suggestion that love might be "beyond" interpellation is an important one. Althusser would have benefited from a better understanding of how the law becomes the object of passionate attachment, a strange scene of love. For the conscience which compels the wayward pedestrian to turn around upon hearing the policeman's address or urges the murderer into the streets in search of the police appears to be driven by a love of the law which can be satisfied only by ritual punishment. To the extent that Althusser gestures toward this analysis, he begins to explain how a subject is formed through the passionate pursuit of the reprimanding recognition of the state. That the subject turns round or rushes 'toward the law suggests that the subject lives in passionate expectation of the law. Such love is not beyond interpellation; rather, it forms the passionate circle in which the subject becomes ensnared by its own state.

The failure of interpellation is clearly to be valued, but to figure that failure in terms that rehabilitate a structure of love outside the domain of the social risks reifying particular social forms of love as eternal psychic facts. It also leaves unexplained the passion that precedes and forms conscience, that precedes and forms the possibility of love, one that accounts for the failure of interpellation fully to constitute the subject it names. Interpellation is "barred" from success not by a structurally permanent form of prohibition (or foreclosure), but by its inability to determine the constitutive field of the human. If conscience is one form that the passionate attachment to existence takes, then the failure of interpellation is to be found precisely in the passionate attachment that also allows it to work. According to the logic of conscience, which fully constrains Althusser, the subject's existence cannot be linguistically guaranteed without passionate attachment to the law. This complicity at once conditions and limits the viability of a critical interrogation of the law. One cannot criticize too far the terms by which one's existence is secured.

But if the discursive possibilities for existence exceed the reprimand voiced by the law, would that not lessen the need to confirm one's guilt and embark on a path of conscientiousness as a way to gain a purchase on identity? What are the conditions under which our very sense of linguistic survival depends upon our willingness to turn back upon ourselves, that is, in which attaining recognizable being requires self-negation, requires existing as a self-negating being in order to attain and preserve a status as "being" at all?

In a Nietzschean vein, such a slave morality may be predicated upon the sober calculation that it is better to "be" enslaved in such a way than not to "be" at all. But the terms that constrain the option to being versus not being "call for" another kind of response. Under what conditions does a law monopolize the terms of existence in so thorough a way? Or is this a theological fantasy of the law? Is there a possibility of being elsewhere or otherwise, without denying our complicity in the law that we oppose? Such possibility would require a different kind of turn, one that, enabled by the law, turns away from the law, resisting its lure of identity, an agency that outruns and counters the conditions of its emergence. Such a turn demands a willingness *not* to be—a critical desubjectivation—in order to expose the law as less powerful than it seems. What forms might linguistic survival take in this desubjectivized domain? How would one know one's existence? Through what terms would it be recognized and recognizable? Such questions cannot be answered here, but they indicate a direction for thinking that is perhaps prior to the question of conscience, namely, the question that preoccupied Spinoza, Nietzsche, and most recently, Giorgio Agamben: How are we to understand the desire to be as a constitutive desire? Resituating conscience and interpellation within such an account, we might then add to this question another: How is such a desire exploited not only by a law in the singular, but by laws of various kinds such that we yield to subordination in order to maintain some sense of social "being"?

In conclusion, Agamben offers us one direction for rethinking ethics along the lines of the desire to be, hence, at a distance from any particular formation of conscience:

if human beings were or had to be this or that substance, this or that destiny, no ethical experience would be possible. . . .

This does not mean, however, that humans are not, and do not have to be, something, that they are simply consigned to nothingness and therefore can freely decide whether to be or not to be, to adopt or not to adopt this or that destiny (nihilism and decisionism coincide at this point). There is in effect something that humans are and have to be, but this is not an essence nor properly a thing: *It is the simple fact of one's own existence as possibility or potentiality.*[20]

Agamben might be read as claiming that this possibility must resolve itself into something, but cannot undo its own status as possibility through such a resolution. Or, rather, we might reread "being" as precisely the potentiality that remains unexhausted by any particular interpellation. Such a failure of interpellation may well undermine the capacity of the subject to "be" in a self-identical sense, but it may also mark the path toward a more open, even more ethical, kind of being, one of or for the future.

Melancholy Gender /
Refused Identification

In grief the world becomes poor and empty; in melancholia
it is the ego itself. —Freud, "Mourning and Melancholia"

How is it then that in melancholia the super-ego can
become a gathering-place for the death instincts?
                                —Freud, *The Ego and the Id*

It may at first seem strange to think of gender as a kind
of melancholy, or as one of melancholy's effects. But let us
remember that in *The Ego and the Id* Freud himself acknowledged that melancholy, the unfinished process of grieving, is
central to the formation of the identifications that form the
ego. Indeed, identifications formed from unfinished grief are
the modes in which the lost object is incorporated and phantasmatically preserved in and as the ego. Consider in conjunc-
tion with this insight Freud's further remark that "the ego is
first and foremost a bodily ego,"[1] not merely a surface, but
"the projection of a surface." Further, this bodily ego assumes
a gendered morphology, so that the bodily ego is also a gendered ego. I hope first to explain the sense in which a melan-

cholic identification is central to the process whereby the ego assumes a gendered character. Second, I want to explore how this analysis of the melancholic formation of gender sheds light on the predicament of living within a culture which can mourn the loss of homosexual attachment only with great difficulty.

Reflecting on his speculations in "Mourning and Melancholia," Freud writes in *The Ego and the Id* that in the earlier essay he had supposed that "an object which was lost has been set up again inside the ego—that is, that an object-cathexis had been replaced by an identification. At that time, however," he continued, "we did not appreciate the full significance of this process and did not know how common and how typical it is. Since then we have come to understand that this kind of substitution has a great share in determining the form taken by the ego and that it makes an essential contribution toward building up what is called its 'character'" (p. 28). Slightly later in the same text, Freud expands this view: "when it happens that a person has to give up a sexual object, there quite often ensues an alteration of his ego which can only be described as a setting up of the object inside the ego, as it occurs in melancholia" (29). He concludes this discussion by speculating that "it may be that this identification is the sole condition under which the id can give up its objects . . . it makes it possible to suppose that the character of the ego is a precipitate of abandoned object-cathexes and that it contains the history of those object-choices" (29). What Freud here calls the "character of the ego" appears to be the sedimentation of objects loved and lost, the archaelogical remainder, as it were, of unresolved grief.

What is perhaps most striking about his formulation here is how it reverses his position in "Mourning and Melancholia" on what it means to resolve grief. In the earlier essay, Freud assumes that grief can be resolved through a de-cathexis, a breaking of attachment, as well as the subsequent making of new attachments. In *The Ego and the Id*, he makes room for the notion that melancholic identification may be a *prerequisite* for letting the object go. By claiming this, he changes what it means to "let an object go," for there is no final breaking of the attachment. There is, rather, the incorporation of the attachment *as* identification, where identification becomes a magical, a psychic form of preserving the object. Insofar as identification is the psychic preserve of the object and such identifications come to form the ego, the lost object continues to haunt and inhabit the ego as one of its constitutive identifications. The lost object is, in that sense, made coextensive with the ego itself. Indeed, one might conclude that melancholic identification permits the loss of the object in the external world precisely because it provides a way to *preserve* the object as part of the ego and, hence, to avert the loss as a complete loss. Here we see that letting the object go means, paradoxically, not full abandonment of the object but transferring the status of the object from external to internal. Giving up the object becomes possible only on the condition of a melancholic internalization or, what might for our purposes turn out to be even more important, a melancholic *incorporation*.

If in melancholia a loss is refused, it is not for that reason abolished. Internalization preserves loss in the psyche; more precisely, the internalization of loss is part of the mechanism of its refusal. If the object can no longer exist in the external world, it will then exist internally, and that internalization will be a way to disavow the loss, to keep it at bay, to stay or postpone the recognition and suffering of loss.

Is there a way in which *gender* identifications or, rather, the identifications that become central to the formation of gender, are produced through melancholic identification? It seems clear that the positions of "masculine" and "feminine," which Freud, in *Three Essays on the Theory of Sexuality* (1905), understood as the effects of laborious and uncertain accomplishment, are established in part through prohibitions which *demand the loss* of certain sexual attachments, and demand as well that those losses *not* be avowed, and *not* be grieved. If the assumption of femininity and the assumption of masculinity proceed through the accomplishment of an always tenuous heterosexuality, we might understand the force of this accomplishment as mandating the abandonment of homosexual attachments or, perhaps more trenchantly, *preempting* the possibility of homosexual attachment, a foreclosure of possibility which produces a domain of homosexuality understood as unlivable passion and ungrievable loss. This heterosexuality is produced not only through implementing the prohibition on incest but, prior to that, by enforcing the prohibition on homosexuality. The oedipal conflict presumes that heterosexual desire has already been *accomplished*, that the distinction between heterosexual and homosexual has been enforced (a distinction which, after all, has no necessity); in this sense, the prohibition on incest presupposes the prohibition on homosexuality, for it presumes the heterosexualization of desire.

To accept this view we must begin by presupposing that masculine and feminine are not dispositions, as Freud sometimes argues, but indeed accomplishments, ones which emerge in tandem with the achievement of heterosexuality. Here Freud articulates a cultural logic whereby gender is achieved and stabilized through heterosexual positioning, and where threats to heterosexuality thus become threats to gender itself. The prevalence of this heterosexual matrix in the construction of gender emerges not only in Freud's text, but in the cultural

forms of life that have absorbed this matrix and are inhabited by everyday forms of gender anxiety. Hence, the fear of
homosexual desire in a woman may induce a panic that she is
losing her femininity, that she is not a woman, that she is no
longer a proper woman, that if she is not quite a man, she is
like one, and hence monstrous in some way. Or in a man, the
terror of homosexual desire may lead to a terror of being construed as feminine, feminized, of no longer being properly a
man, of being a "failed" man, or being in some sense a figure
of monstrosity or abjection.

I would argue that phenomenologically there are many
ways of experiencing gender and sexuality that do not reduce
to this equation, that do not presume that gender is stabilized
through the installation of a firm heterosexuality, but for the
moment I want to invoke this stark and hyperbolic construction of the relation between gender and sexuality in order to
think through the question of ungrieved and ungreivable loss
in the formation of what we might call the gendered character
of the ego.

Consider that gender is acquired at least in part through
the repudiation of homosexual attachments; the girl becomes
a girl through being subject to a prohibition which bars the
mother as an object of desire and installs that barred object as
a part of the ego, indeed, as a melancholic identification. Thus
the identification contains within it both the prohibition and
the desire, and so embodies the ungrieved loss of the homosexual cathexis. If one is a girl to the extent that one does not
want a girl, then wanting a girl will bring being a girl into
question; within this matrix, homosexual desire thus panics
gender.

Heterosexuality is cultivated through prohibitions, and
these prohibitions take as one of their objects homosexual at-

tachments, thereby forcing the loss of those attachments.[2] If the girl is to transfer love from her father to a substitute object, she must, according to Freudian logic, first renounce love for her mother, and renounce it in such a way that both the aim and the object are foreclosed. She must not transfer that homosexual love onto a substitute feminine figure, but renounce the possibility of homosexual attachment itself. Only on this condition does a heterosexual aim become established as what some call a sexual orientation. Only on the condition of this foreclosure of homosexuality can the father and substitutes for him become objects of desire, and the mother become the uneasy site of identification.

Becoming a "man" within this logic requires repudiating femininity as a precondition for the heterosexualization of sexual desire and its fundamental ambivalence. If a man becomes heterosexual by repudiating the feminine, where could that repudiation live except in an identification which his heterosexual career seeks to deny? Indeed, the desire for the feminine is marked by that repudiation: he wants the woman he would never be. He wouldn't be caught dead being her: therefore he wants her. She is his repudiated identification (a repudiation he sustains as at once identification and the object of his desire). One of the most anxious aims of his desire will be to elaborate the difference between him and her, and he will seek to discover and install proof of that difference. His wanting will be haunted by a dread of being what he wants, so that his wanting will also always be a kind of dread. Precisely because what is repudiated and hence lost is preserved as a repudiated identification, this desire will attempt to overcome an identification which can never be complete.

Indeed, he will not identify with her, and he will not desire another man. That refusal to desire, that sacrifice of desire under the force of prohibition, will incorporate homosexuality as an identification with masculinity. But this masculinity will be haunted by the love it cannot grieve, and before I suggest how this might be true, I'd like to situate the kind of writing that I have been offering as a certain cultural engagement with psychoanalytic theory that belongs neither to the fields of psychology nor to psychoanalysis, but which nevertheless seeks to establish an intellectual relationship to those enterprises.

Thus far, I have been offering something like an exegesis of a certain psychoanalytic logic, one that appears in some psychoanalytic texts but which these texts and others also sometimes contest. I make no empirical claims, nor attempt a survey of current psychoanalytic scholarship on gender, sexuality, or melancholy. I want merely to suggest what I take to be some productive convergences between Freud's thinking on ungrieved and ungrievable loss and the predicament of living in a culture which can mourn the loss of homosexual attachment only with great difficulty.

This problematic is made all the more acute when we consider the ravages of AIDS, and the task of finding a public occasion and language in which to grieve this seemingly endless number of deaths. More generally, this problem makes itself felt in the uncertainty with which homosexual love and loss is regarded: is it regarded as a "true" love, a "true" loss, a love and loss worthy and capable of being grieved, and thus worthy and capable of having been lived? Or is it a love and a loss haunted by the specter of a certain unreality, a certain unthinkability, the double disavowal of the "I never loved her, and I never lost her," uttered by a woman, the "I never loved him, I never lost him," uttered by a man? Is this the "never-never" that supports the naturalized surface of heterosexual life as well as its pervasive melancholia? Is it the disavowal of

loss by which sexual formation, including gay sexual formation, proceeds?

If we accept the notion that the prohibition on homosexuality operates throughout a largely heterosexual culture as
one of its defining operations, then the loss of homosexual objects and aims (not simply this person of the same gender,
but *any* person of the same gender) would appear to be foreclosed from the start. I say "foreclosed" to suggest that this is
a preemptive loss, a mourning for unlived possibilities. If this
love is from the start out of the question, then it cannot happen, and if it does, it certainly did not. If it does, it happens
only under the official sign of its prohibition and disavowal.[3]
When certain kinds of losses are compelled by a set of culturally prevalent prohibitions, we might expect a culturally
prevalent form of melancholia, one which signals the internalization of the ungrieved and ungrievable homosexual cathexis. And where there is no public recognition or discourse
through which such a loss might be named and mourned,
then melancholia takes on cultural dimensions of contemporary consequence. Of course, it comes as no surprise that the
more hyperbolic and defensive a masculine identification, the
more fierce the ungrieved homosexual cathexis. In this sense,
we might understand both "masculinity" and "femininity" as
formed and consolidated through identifications which are in
part composed of disavowed grief.

If we accept the notion that heterosexuality naturalizes
itself by insisting on the radical otherness of homosexuality,
then heterosexual identity is purchased through a melancholic
incorporation of the love that it disavows: the man who insists
upon the coherence of his heterosexuality will claim that he
never loved another man, and hence never lost another man.
That love, that attachment becomes subject to a double dis-

avowal, a never having loved, and a never having lost. This "never-never" thus founds the heterosexual subject, as it were; it is an identity based upon the refusal to avow an attachment and, hence, the refusal to grieve.

There is perhaps a more culturally instructive way of describing this scenario, for it is not simply a matter of an individual's unwillingness to avow and hence to grieve homosexual attachments. When the prohibition against homosexuality is culturally pervasive, then the "loss" of homosexual love is precipitated through a prohibition which is repeated and ritualized throughout the culture. What ensues is a culture of gender melancholy in which masculinity and femininity emerge as the traces of an ungrieved and ungrievable love; indeed, where masculinity and femininity within the heterosexual matrix are strengthened through the repudiations that they perform. In opposition to a conception of sexuality which is said to "express" a gender, gender itself is here understood to be composed of precisely what remains inarticulate in sexuality.

If we understand gender melancholy in this way, then perhaps we can make sense of the peculiar phenomenon whereby homosexual desire becomes a source of guilt. In "Mourning and Melancholia" Freud argues that melancholy is marked by the experience of self-beratement. He writes, "If one listens carefully to the many and various self-accusations of the melancholic, one cannot in the end avoid the impression that often the most violent of them are hardly at all applicable to the patient himself, but that with insignificant modifications they do fit someone else, some person whom the patient loves, has loved or ought to love . . . the self-reproaches are reproaches against a loved object which have been shifted on to the patient's own ego."[4]

Freud goes on to conjecture that the conflict with the other which remains unresolved at the time the other is lost re-emerges in the psyche as a way of continuing the quarrel. Indeed, anger at the other is doubtless exacerbated by the death or departure which occasions the loss. But this anger is turned inward and becomes the substance of self-beratement.

In "On Narcissism," Freud links the experience of guilt with the turning back into the ego of homosexual libido.[5] Putting aside the question of whether libido can be homosexual or heterosexual, we might rephrase Freud and consider guilt as the turning back into the ego of homosexual attachment. If the loss becomes a renewed scene of conflict, and if the aggression that follows from that loss cannot be articulated or externalized, then it rebounds upon the ego itself, in the form of a super-ego. This will eventually lead Freud to link melancholic identification with the agency of the super-ego in *The Ego and the Id*, but already in "On Narcissism" we have some sense of how guilt is wrought from ungrievable homosexuality.

The ego is said to become impoverished in melancholia, but it appears as poor precisely through the workings of self-beratement. The ego-ideal, what Freud calls the "measure" against which the ego is judged by the super-ego, is precisely the ideal of social rectitude defined over and against homosexuality. "This ideal," Freud writes, "has a social side: it is also the common ideal of a family, a class or a nation. It not only binds the narcissistic libido, but also a considerable amount of the person's homosexual libido, which in this way becomes turned back into the ego. The dissatisfaction due to the non-fulfillment of this ideal liberates homosexual libido, which is transformed into a sense of guilt (dread of the community)" (81).

But the movement of this "transformation" is not altogether

clear. After all, Freud will argue in *Civilization and Its Discontents* that these social ideals are transformed into a sense of guilt through a kind of internalization which is not, ultimately, mimetic. In "On Narcissism," it is not that one treats oneself as harshly as one was treated but rather that the aggression toward the ideal and its unfulfillability is turned inward, and this self-aggression becomes the primary structure of conscience: "by means of identification [the child] takes the unattackable authority into himself" (86).

In this sense, in melancholia the super-ego can become a gathering place for the death instincts. As such, it is not necessarily the same as those instincts or their effect. In this way, melancholia attracts the death instincts to the super-ego, the death instincts being understood as a regressive striving toward organic equilibrium, and the self-beratement of the super-ego being understood to make use of that regressive striving for its own purposes. Melancholy is both the refusal of grief and the incorporation of loss, a miming of the death it cannot mourn. Yet the incorporation of death draws upon the death instincts to such a degree that we might well wonder whether the two can be separated from one another, whether analytically or phenomenologically.

The prohibition on homosexuality preempts the process of grief and prompts a melancholic identification which effectively turns homosexual desire back upon itself. This turning back upon itself is precisely the action of self-beratement and guilt. Significantly, homosexuality is *not* abolished but preserved, though preserved precisely in the prohibition on homosexuality. In *Civilization and Its Discontents*, Freud makes clear that conscience requires the continuous sacrifice or renunciation of instinct to produce the peculiar satisfaction that conscience requires; conscience is never assuaged by renunciation, but is paradoxically strengthened ("renunciation breeds intolerance").[6] Renunciation does not abolish the instinct; it deploys the instinct for its own purposes, so that prohibition, and the lived experience of prohibition as repeated renunciation, is nourished precisely by the instinct that it renounces. In this scenario, renunciation requires the very homosexuality that it condemns, not as its external object, but as its own most treasured source of sustenance. The act of renouncing homosexuality thus paradoxically strengthens homosexuality, but it strengthens homosexuality precisely *as* the power of renunciation. Renunciation becomes the aim and vehicle of satisfaction. And it is, we might conjecture, precisely the fear of setting homosexuality loose from this circuit of renunciation that so terrifies the guardians of masculinity in the U.S. military. What would masculinity "be" without this aggressive circuit of renunciation from which it is wrought? Gays in the military threaten to undo masculinity only because this masculinity is made of repudiated homosexuality.[7]

Some suggestions I made in *Bodies That Matter*[8] can facilitate the transition from the consideration of melancholia as a specifically psychic economy to the production of the circuitry of melancholia as part of the operation of regulatory power. If melancholia designates a sphere of attachment that is not explicitly produced as an object of discourse, then it erodes the operation of language that not only posits objects, but regulates and normalizes objects through that positing. If melancholia appears at first to be a form of containment, a way of internalizing an attachment that is barred from the world, it also establishes the psychic conditions for regarding "the world" itself as contingently organized through certain kinds of foreclosures.[9]

Having described a melancholy produced through the compulsory production of heterosexuality, thus, a heterosexual melancholy that one might read in the workings of gender itself, I want now to suggest that rigid forms of gender and sexual identification, whether homosexual or heterosexual, appear to spawn forms of melancholy. I would like first to reconsider the theory of gender as performative that I elaborated in *Gender Trouble*, and then to turn to the question of gay melancholia and the political consequences of ungrievable loss.

There I argued that gender is performative, by which I meant that no gender is "expressed" by actions, gestures, or speech, but that the performance of gender produces retroactively the illusion that there is an inner gender core. That is, the performance of gender retroactively produces the effect of some true or abiding feminine essence or disposition, so that one cannot use an expressive model for thinking about gender. Moreover, I argued that gender is produced as a ritualized repetition of conventions, and that this ritual is socially compelled in part by the force of a compulsory heterosexuality. In this context, I would like to return to the question of drag to explain in clearer terms how I understand psychoanalysis to be linked with gender performativity, and how I take performativity to be linked with melancholia.

It is not enough to say that gender is performed, or that the meaning of gender can be derived from its performance, whether or not one wants to rethink performance as a compulsory social ritual. Clearly there are workings of gender that do not "show" in what is performed as gender, and to reduce the psychic workings of gender to the literal performance of gender would be a mistake. Psychoanalysis insists that the opacity of the unconscious sets limits to the exteriorization of the psyche. It also argues—rightly, I think—that what is exteriorized or performed can only be understood by reference to what is barred from performance, what cannot or will not be performed.

The relation between drag performances and gender performativity in *Gender Trouble* goes something like this: when a man is performing drag as a woman, the "imitation" that drag is said to be is taken as an "imitation" of femininity, but the "femininity" that he imitates is not understood as being itself an imitation. Yet if one considers that gender is acquired, that it is assumed in relation to ideals which are never quite inhabited by anyone, then femininity is an ideal which everyone always and only "imitates." Thus, drag imitates the imitative structure of gender, revealing gender itself to be an imitation. However attractive this formulation may have seemed, it didn't address the question of how certain forms of disavowal and repudiation come to organize the performance of gender. How is the phenomenon of gender melancholia to be related to the practice of gender performativity?

Moreover, given the iconographic figure of the melancholic drag queen, one might ask whether there is not a dissatisfied longing in the mimetic incorporation of gender that is drag. Here one might ask also after the disavowal which occasions the performance and which performance might be said to enact, where performance engages "acting out" in the psychoanalytic sense. If melancholia in Freud's sense is the effect of an ungrieved loss,[10] performance, understood as "acting out," may be related to the problem of unacknowledged loss. If there is an ungrieved loss in drag performance, perhaps it is a loss that is refused and incorporated in the performed identification, one which reiterates a gendered idealization and its radical uninhabitability. This is, then, neither a territorialization of the feminine by the masculine nor a sign of the essential plasticity of gender. It suggests that the performance allegorizes a loss it cannot grieve, allegorizes the incorporative fantasy of melancholia whereby an object is phantasmatically taken in or on as a way of refusing to let it go. Gender itself might be understood in part as the "acting out" of unresolved grief.

The above analysis is a risky one because it suggests that for a "man" performing femininity, or for a "woman" performing masculinity (the latter is always, in effect, to perform a little less, given that femininity is cast as the spectacular gender), there is an attachment to—and a loss and refusal of—the figure of femininity by the man, or the figure of masculinity by the woman. It is important to underscore that, although drag is an effort to negotiate cross-gendered identification, cross-gendered identification is not the only paradigm for thinking about homosexuality, merely one among others. Drag allegorizes some set of melancholic incorporative fantasies that stabilize *gender*. Not only are a vast number of drag performers straight, but it would be a mistake to think that homosexuality is best explained through the performativity that is drag. What does seem useful in this analysis, however, is that drag exposes or allegorizes the mundane psychic and performative practices by which heterosexualized genders form themselves through renouncing the *possibility* of homosexuality, a foreclosure which produces both a field of heterosexual objects and a domain of those whom it would be impossible to love. Drag thus allegorizes *heterosexual melancholy*, the melancholy by which a masculine gender is formed from the refusal to grieve the masculine as a possibility of love; a feminine gender is formed (taken on, assumed) through the incorporative fantasy by which the feminine is excluded as a possible object of love, an exclusion never grieved, but "preserved" through heightened feminine identification. In this sense, the "truest" lesbian melancholic is the strictly straight woman, and the "truest" gay male melancholic is the strictly straight man.

What drag does expose, however, is that in the "normal" constitution of gender presentation, the gender that is performed is constituted by a set of disavowed attachments, identifications which constitute a different domain of the "unperformable." Indeed, what constitutes the *sexually* unperformable may—but need not—be performed as *gender identification*.[11] To the extent that homosexual attachments remain unacknowledged within normative heterosexuality, they are not merely constituted as desires which emerge and subsequently become prohibited; rather, these desires are proscribed from the start. And when they do emerge on the far side of the censor, they may well carry the mark of impossibility with them, performing, as it were, as the impossible within the possible. As such, they will not be attachments that can be openly grieved. This is, then, less a *refusal* to grieve (the Mitscherlich formulation that accents the choice involved) than a preemption of grief performed by the absence of cultural conventions for avowing the loss of homosexual love. And this absence produces a culture of heterosexual melancholy, one which can be read in the hyperbolic identifications by which mundane heterosexual masculinity and femininity confirm themselves. The straight man *becomes* (mimes, cites, appropriates, assumes the status of) the man he "never" loved and "never" grieved; the straight woman *becomes* the woman she "never" loved and "never" grieved. It is in this sense, then, that what is most apparently performed as gender is the sign and symptom of a pervasive disavowal.

Gay melancholia, however, also contains anger that can be translated into political expression. It is precisely to counter this pervasive cultural risk of gay melancholia (what the newspapers generalize as "depression") that there has been an insistent publicization and politicization of grief over those who have died from AIDS. The Names Project Quilt is exemplary, ritualizing and repeating the name itself as a way of publically avowing limitless loss.[12]

Insofar as the grief remains unspeakable, the rage over the loss can redouble by virtue of remaining unavowed. And if that rage is publically proscribed, the melancholic effects of such a proscription can achieve suicidal proportions. The emergence of collective institutions for grieving are thus crucial to survival, to reassembling community, to rearticulating kinship, to reweaving sustaining relations. Insofar as they involve the publicization and dramatization of death—as in the case of "die-ins" by Queer Nation—they call for being read as life-affirming rejoinders to the dire psychic consequences of a grieving process culturally thwarted and proscribed.

Melancholy can work, however, within homosexuality in specific ways that call for rethinking. Within the formation of gay and lesbian identity, there may be an effort to disavow a constitutive relationship to heterosexuality. When this disavowal is understood as a political necessity in order to *specify* gay and lesbian identity over and against its ostensible opposite, heterosexuality, that cultural practice paradoxically culminates in a weakening of the very constituency it is meant to unite. Not only does such a strategy attribute a false and monolithic status to heterosexuality, but it misses the political opportunity to work on the weakness in heterosexual subjectivation and to refute the logic of mutual exclusion by which heterosexism proceeds. Moreover, a full-scale denial of the interrelationship can constitute a rejection of heterosexuality that is to some degree an identification *with* a rejected heterosexuality. Important to this economy, however, is the refusal to recognize this identification that is, as it were, already made, a refusal which absently designates the domain of a specifically gay melancholia, a loss which cannot be recognized and, hence, cannot be mourned. For a gay or lesbian identity position to sustain its appearance as coherent, heterosexuality must remain in that rejected and repudiated place. Paradoxically, its heterosexual *remains* must be *sustained* precisely through insisting on the seamless coherence of a specifically gay identity. Here it should become clear that a radical refusal to identify suggests that on some level an identification has already taken place, an identification has been made and disavowed, whose symptomatic appearance is the insistence, the overdetermination of the identification that is, as it were, worn on the body that shows.

This raises the political question of the cost of articulating a coherent identity position by producing, excluding, and repudiating a domain of abjected specters that threaten the arbitrarily closed domain of subject positions. Perhaps only by risking the *incoherence* of identity is connection possible, a political point that correlates with Leo Bersani's insight that only the decentered subject is available to desire.[13] What cannot be avowed as a constitutive identification for any given subject position runs the risk not only of becoming externalized in a degraded form, but repeatedly repudiated and subject to a policy of disavowal.

The logic of repudiation that I've charted here is in some ways a hyperbolic theory, a logic in drag, as it were, which overstates the case, but overstates it for a reason. There is no necessary reason for identification to oppose desire, or for desire to be fueled by repudiation. This remains true for heterosexuality and homosexuality alike, and for forms of bi-sexuality that take themselves to be composite forms of each. Indeed, we are made all the more fragile under the pressure of such rules, and all the more mobile when ambivalence and loss are given a dramatic language in which to do their acting out.

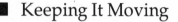 Keeping It Moving

Commentary on Judith Butler's
"Melancholy Gender / Refused
Identification"

ADAM PHILLIPS

Ends of sentences and other pauses only come when we run
out of time or hope.
— Carolyn Creedon, *The Best American Poetry*

If, as Freud suggests, character is constituted by identification—the ego likening itself to what it once loved—then
character is close to caricature, an imitation of an imitation.[1]
Like the artists Plato wanted to ban, we are making copies of
copies, but unlike Plato's artists we have no original, only an
infinite succession of likenesses to someone who, to all intents
and purposes, does not exist. Freud's notion of character is a
parody of a Platonic work of art; his theory of character formation through identification makes a mockery of character
as in any way substantive. The ego is always dressing up for
somewhere to go. Insofar as being is being like, there can be

no place for True selves or core gender identities. After all, my sense of authenticity can come only from the senses of authenticity in my culture. In this context, my True Self is more accurately described as my Preferred Self (or Selves). I am the performer of my conscious and unconscious preferences.

Lacan's mirror-stage is a testament to the havoc wreaked by mimetic forms of development; and Mikkel Borch-Jacobsen and Leo Bersani in particular have exposed the violence and tautology of Freud's theory of identification, the mutual implication and complicity involved in being like.[2] As Judith Butler's sobering essay shows, this critical concept of identification is the nexus for a number of contentious issues in contemporary theory; it invites us to wonder what we use other people for and how other they are. In fact, it forces us to confront the question that exercised Freud and that object relations and relational psychoanalysis take for granted; in what sense do we have what we prefer to call relationships with each other?

When Freud proposed that the object was merely "soldered" on to the instinct, that our primary commitment was to our desire and not to its target, he implied that we are not attached to each other in the ways we like to think.[3] Freud glimpsed in the *Interpretation of Dreams* the ego's potential for promiscuous mobility; dreams in particular revealed that psychic life was astonishingly mobile and adventurous even if lived life was not. (Very few people are actively bisexual yet everyone is psychically bisexual.) Freud had both to explain this disparity—that we do not have the courage, as it were, of our primary process—and also to find a way, in theory, of grounding the Faustian ego, defining its loyalties when they sometimes seemed unreliable. The ego certainly seemed shifty in its allegiances, and so it was with some relief that Freud turned to mourning, which seemed to reveal that the ego is grounded in its relationship with loved and hated others.[4] Mourning is immensely reassuring because it convinces us of something we might otherwise doubt; our attachment to others. The protracted painfulness of mourning confirms something that psychoanalysis had put into question: how intransigently devoted we are to the people we love and hate. Despite the evidence of our dreams, our capacity for infinite substitution is meager. In this sense, mourning has been a ballast for the more radical possibilities of psychoanalysis. It is the rock, so to speak, on which Prometheus founders.

It might at first seem more accurate to say that, for Freud, it was the Oedipus complex that both constituted and set limits to the exorbitance of the ego. But it is, as Klein has shown, the mourning entailed in the so-called resolution of the Oedipus complex that consolidates the ego. Without mourning for primary objects there is no way out of the magic circle of the family. Indeed, partly through the work of Klein, mourning has provided the foundation for development in most versions of psychoanalysis; so much so, in fact, that mourning has acquired the status of a quasi-religious concept in psychoanalysis. Analysts believe in mourning; if a patient were to claim, as Emerson once did, that mourning was "shallow" he or she would be considered to be "out of touch" with something or other. It is as though a capacity for mourning, with all that it implies, constitutes the human community. We can no more imagine a world without bereavement than we can imagine a world without punishment.

I think that, somewhat along these lines, Judith Butler is trying to use mourning to give some gravity, in both senses, to her exhilarating notion of gender as performative. What is remarkable about her essay is that she manages to do this

without the argument's degenerating into the more coercive
pieties that talk about grief usually brings in its wake. Mourning makes moralists of us all. There will never be more gender
identities than we can invent and perform. We should not be
celebrating those people, many of whom are psychoanalysts,
who, in the name of Truth, or Psychic Health, or Maturity,
seek to limit the repertoire.

It is now a cliché, in theory if not in practice, that all versions of gender identity are conflictual and therefore problematic. What Butler is proposing with her notion of a melancholic
identification, a "culture of gender melancholy in which masculinity and femininity emerge as the traces of an ungrieved
and ungrievable love," is a new version of an old question
about gender identity. Why are homosexual attachments—
the inappropriately named "negative" Oedipus complex—described, even if not originally experienced, aversively? Why
are these manifestly passionate loves disavowed, made un-
mournable, repudiated, and then punished when witnessed
in others? At the least, it seems clear from Butler's convinc-
ing account that the culturally pervasive hostility—both inter-
and intrapsychically—to homosexuality is based on envy. If
some heterosexuals in pre-AIDS times were explicitly envious
of the promiscuity of homosexuals—why can't WE cruise?—
heterosexuals now may be more likely to envy simply the inti-
macy that some people are free to indulge and elaborate with
people of the same sex. But if, as Butler suggests, "masculinity" and "femininity" are formed and consolidated through
identifications that are composed in part of disavowed grief,
what would it be like to live in a world that acknowledged
and sanctioned such grief, that allowed us, as it were, the full
course of our bereavement of disowned or renounced gender identities? What would have to happen in the so-called

psychoanalytic community for an ethos to be created in which patients were encouraged to mourn the loss of all their repressed gender identities?

These seem to me to be questions of considerable interest, provided they do not entail the idealization of mourning—its use as a spurious redemptive practice, as a kind of ersatz cure for repression or the anguishes of uncertainty. If the convinced heterosexual man, in Butler's words, "becomes subject to a double disavowal, a never-having-loved and a never-having-lost," the homosexual attachment, is it therefore to become integral to the psychoanalytic project to analyze, or engineer the undoing of this disavowal if the heterosexual man claims to be relatively untroubled by it? To me, the absolute plausibility of Butler's argument poses some telling clinical quandaries. Who, for example, decides what constitutes a problem for the patient? And by what criteria? Assumed heterosexuality is every bit as much of a "problem" as any other assumed position (all symptoms, after all, are states of conviction). Certainly Butler's paper reminds us of the cost, the deprivation, in all gender identities, not to mention the terror informing these desperate measures. "There is," Butler writes, "no necessary reason for identification to oppose desire, or for desire to be fueled by repudiation." But there is, of course, a necessary reason by a certain kind of psychoanalytic logic. In Freud's view, we become what we cannot have, and we desire (and punish) what we are compelled to disown. But why these choices—why can't we do both and something else as well?—and why are they the choices?

These are the issues opened up in Butler's *Gender Trouble*. The essentially performative, constructed nature of gender identity makes all constraints of the repertoire seem factitious and unnecessarily oppressive. But just as every performance is subsidized by an inhibition elsewhere, so there is no identity, however compelling the performance, without suffering. If the idea of performance frees identity into states of (sometimes willed) possibility, mourning refers those same identities back to their unconscious histories, with their repetitions and their waste; those parameters that seemingly thwart our options. Mourning and performance—and the performances that constitute our sense of mourning—seem usefully twinned. Without the idea of performance, mourning becomes literalized as Truth—our deepest act; without the idea of mourning, performance becomes an excessive demand—pretend there's no unconscious, then pretend what you like. "I believe in all sincerity," Valéry wrote, "that if each man were not able to live a number of lives beside his own, he would not be able to live his own life."[5] Valéry's ironic sincerity—from which of his lives is he speaking?—invites us, like Butler, to multiply our versions of self as some kind of psychic necessity; as though we might not be able to bear the loss of not doing so. But how many lives can the analyst recognize in, or demand of, his patient, and what are the constraints on this recognition that so easily becomes a demand?

In analysis, of course, it is not only the patient's gender identities that are at stake. Both the analyst and her patient are working to sustain their desire, and desire—both intra- and interpsychically—depends on difference. There always has to be something else, something sufficiently (or apparently) other. The specter of Aphanisis, Jones's repressed concept of the death of desire, haunts the process. But though desire depends on difference, we only like the differences we like; the set of desirable or tolerable differences, desire-sustaining difference, is never infinite for anyone. Psychoanalysis is about where we draw these constitutive lines. Any clinician is only too conscious of the constraints, the unconscious constraints, on possibility that are called symptoms (and from a different perspective are called the Oedipus complex). But, of course, what is possible in analysis, or anywhere else, is dictated by our theoretical paradigms, by the languages we choose to speak about our practice. Despite boasts to the contrary —psychoanalysis, the Impossible Profession and the like— psychoanalysis is only as difficult as we make it.

From a clinical point of view, Butler's initial political voluntarism in *Gender Trouble* would have made analysts wary. But there is no obvious reason why analysts in their practice have to be less imaginative than Butler is asking them to be in "Melancholy Gender." The analyst who believes in the unconscious can hardly set himself up as a representative of the authentic life even though the language he uses to talk about his job is full of the jargon of authenticity (integrity, honesty, truth, self, instinct). The language of performance may be too easy to dismiss clinically as evasive, in a way that is blind to the theatricality of the analytic situation. Butler's use of identification puts the notion of the performative back into the analytic frame; what is more surprising is that she has been able to use mourning as a way of nuancing the theatricality that is integral to our making of identities, our making ourselves up through loss. It is fortunate that writers are interested in psychoanalysis because, unlike analysts, they are free to think up thoughts unconstrained by the hypnotic effect of clinical practice. Good performers, like musicians or sportspeople or analysts, are often not that good at talking about what they do, partly because they are the ones who do it.

And the doing it, of course, like the living of any life, involves acknowledging, in one way or another, that there are only two sexes. Though this, in and of itself, says nothing about the possible repertoire of gender identities. The logic of Butler's argument, the kind of instructive incoherence she finds in Freud, recuperates a sense of possibility for analytic practice. And yet the very lucidity of Butler's essay also prompts another kind of reflection. It can sometimes seem a shame that there are only two sexes, not least because we use this difference as a paradigm to do so much work for us (the differences between the sexes are, of course, more exciting, or more articulable, than the differences between a live body and a dead body). There is a kind of intellectual melancholy in the loss of a third sex that never existed and so can never be mourned; this third, irrational sex that would break the spell (or the logic) of the two, and that is one of the child's formative and repressed fantasies about himself or herself. (There is a link between this magical solution to the primal scene and fantasies of synthesis and redemption.) What Freud called primary process is, after all, the erasing of mutual exclusion, a logic defying logic. This form of generosity (and radicalism) is not always available, it seems, to our secondary-process selves.

Starting with two sexes, as we must—described as opposites or alternatives or complements—locks us into a logic, a binary system that often seems remote from lived and spoken experience and is complicit with the other binary pairs—inside/outside, primary process/secondary process, sadism/masochism, and so on—that are such a misleading part of psychoanalytic language. We should be speaking of paradoxes and spectrums, not contradictions and mutual exclusion. Every child rightly wants to know whether there is a position beyond exclusion or difference or separateness—a world in which leaving and being left out disappears, an idea taken up at a different level in utopian socialism, which aims at a society without margins and therefore without humiliation.

In thinking about gender, or any of the so-called identities, it seems to be extremely difficult to find a picture or a story that no longer needs the idea of exclusion. And Butler's theoretical descriptions reflect this. There seems to be something bewitching, certainly in psychoanalytic theory, about the idea —and the experience—of evacuation and of the kinds of definition that the idea of inside and outside can give us (in relatively recent psychoanalytic history Balint was asking whether the fish was in the water or the water in the fish). Obviously, the vocabulary of difference—the means of establishing those intra- and interpsychic boundaries and limits which psychoanalysis promotes—is, by definition, far more extensive than the language of sameness (the same, of course, is not only the identical). We can talk about difference—in a sense, that's what talk is about—but sameness makes us mute, dull, or repetitive. And to talk about homosexuality exclusively in terms of sameness is to compound the muddle. Sameness, like difference, is a (motivated) fantasy, not a natural fact. The language of boundaries that psychoanalysis is so intent on, and that makes possible notions of identification and mourning, promotes a specific set of assumptions about what a person is and can be. It is a picture of a person informed by the languages of purity and property, what Mary Douglas more exactly called purity and danger. It may be more useful to talk about gradations and blurring rather than contours and outlines when we plot our stories about gender.[6] Butler's language of performance keeps definition on the move, which is where it is anyway. Mourning slows things down.

■ Reply to Adam Phillips's
Commentary on
"Melancholy Gender /
Refused Identification"

Adam Phillips's welcome commentary confirms that there
might be a dialogue, even perhaps a psychoanalytic one,
between a clinical and a speculative perspective on questions
of gender, melancholia, and performativity. Clearly the positions here are not as "staked out" as is often the case, for
Phillips is himself both a clinician and a speculative thinker,
and thus furthers the doubly dimensioned writing inaugurated
by Freud. Indeed, what might at first seem a strict opposition—the clinician, on the one hand, and the cultural theorist
of gender, on the other—is broken down and reconfigured in
the course of this exchange, and it is as much the content of
his claims as the movement of his own thinking which makes
me want to reconsider the oppositional framing and thinking
which seems, luckily, not to be able to sustain itself here. My
reply will focus first on the question of whether melancholy
is rightly understood to oppose or to temper notions of gen-

der performativity, and second, on whether sexual difference is an opposition that is as stable as it might appear.

Phillips suggests that the consideration of melancholic incorporation tempers the voluntarism of the position associated with gender performativity that has emerged in the reception of *Gender Trouble*. On the one hand, there appears to be a repudiated and unresolved knot of grief, and on the other, a self-conscious subject who, in a Sartrian vein, creates itself anew again and again. But what if the terms of this opposition are not quite as stable as they seem? Consider that the irresolution of melancholia is tied to the check placed upon aggression against the lost other, that the idealization of the other that accompanies self-beratement in melancholia is precisely the routing against the ego of aggression toward the other which is prohibited from being expressed directly. The prohibition works in the service of an idealization, but it also works in the service of an idealization of grief as a pure or sacred practice. The melancholic, barred from aggressive expression, begins to mime and incorporate the lost one, refusing the loss through that incorporative strategy, "continuing the quarrel" with the other, but now in the form of an intrapsychic self-beratement. But this process is not only intrapsychic, for symptomatic expression is precisely the return of what is excluded in the process of idealization. What is the place of "acting out" in relation to symptomatic expression, especially when beratement escapes the intrapsychic circuit to emerge in displaced and externalized forms? Is this kind of "acting out," which often takes the form of a pantomime, not the very venue for an aggression that refuses to remain locked up in the circuit of self-beratement, an aggression that breaks out of that circuit only to heap itself, through displacement, on objects which signify the resonance, the remains, of the lost other? In this sense, what is performed as a consequence of melancholia is not a voluntary act, but an acting out motivated—in part—by an unowned aggression.

How does this account work in the context of gender melancholia? If I acquire my gender by repudiating my love for one of my own gender, then that repudiation lives on in the acting out of my gender and asks to be read as rivalry, aggression, idealization, and melancholia. If I am a woman to the extent that I have never loved one, both aggression and shame are locked into that "never," that "no way," which suggests that whatever gender I am is threatened fundamentally by the return of the love rendered unthinkable by that defensive "never." Therefore what I act, indeed, what I "choose," has something profoundly unchosen in it that runs through the course of that "performance." Here the notion of gender performativity calls for psychoanalytic rethinking through the notion of "acting out," as it emerges in the articulation of melancholia and in the pantomimic response to loss whereby the lost other is incorporated in the formative identifications of the ego.

Phillips is right to warn psychoanalysis against an idealization of mourning itself, the sacralization of mourning as the consummate psychoanalytic ritual. It is as if psychoanalysis as a practice risks becoming afflicted with the very suffering it seeks to know. The resolution of grief becomes unthinkable in a situation in which our various losses become the condition for psychoanalysis as a practice of interminable mourning. But what breaks the hold of grief except the cultivation of the aggression grief holds at bay against the means by which it is held at bay? Part of what sustains and extends the period of mourning is precisely the prohibition against expressing aggression toward what is lost—in part *because* that lost one has abandoned us, and in the sacralization of the object, we exclude the possibility of raging against that abandonment. What are the affirmative consequences of mimetic acting out as it works, within a psychoanalytic frame, to theatricalize that aggression without ethical consequence, and to articulate, for the purposes of self-reflection, through a set of "acts" the logic of repudiation by which they are motivated? Isn't it then the case that such theatricality might work as a psychoanalytic notion and not only as that which must be corrected or tempered by psychoanalysis? Wouldn't that be one way to counter the idealization of mourning (itself a symptom of mourning) which commits psychoanalysis to the sober work of permanent mourning? To what extent is that effect of "permanence" the result of the force of repudiation itself, aggression in the service of a self-berating bind typical of melancholia?

Phillips asks another set of questions, which seem also to work within a certain oppositional frame which may be less oppositional than at first appears. He rephrases my question appropriately when he queries whether there is a necessary reason for identification to oppose desire or for desire to be fueled by repudiation. He claims that within the psychoanalytic framework there are good reasons, and that every position taken up and every desire determined engages a psychic conflict. This follows from the fact that there are always losses, refusals, and sacrifices to be made along the way to having the ego or character formed or having desire disposed in any determinate direction. This seems right. But perhaps there is a way of developing a typology of "refusal" and "exclusion" that might help us distinguish between what is rigorously repudiated and foreclosed, and what happens to be less rigidly or permanently declined. Surely there is, say, a way of accounting for homosexuality which presupposes that it is rooted in an unconscious repudiation of heterosexuality and which, in making that presumption, determines repudiated heterosexuality to be the unconscious "truth" of lived homosexuality. But is such a presumption about repudiation necessary to account for the trajectory of lived homosexuality? Could there be equally compelling accounts of unconscious motivations that account for homosexuality which do not assume the repudiated status of heterosexuality in its formation? And what of those homosexuals who do not rigorously oppose heterosexuality either intrapsychically or interpsychically, but who are nevertheless relatively determined in the directionality of their desire? Perhaps the economy of desire always works through refusal and loss of some kind, but it is not as a consequence an economy structured by a logic of non-contradiction. Isn't this kind of postcontradictory psychic mobility what is desired psychoanalytically, and what Freud sought to circumscribe through reference to the bisexedness of the psyche? Is this mobility not a sign that a rigorously instituted logic of repudiation is not, after all, necessary for psychic survival?

It seems to me that we must accept, as Phillips rightly counsels us to do, that there is no "position beyond exclusion—or difference, or separateness" and no "world in which leaving and being left out disappears." But does this acceptance commit us to the position that "sex" is a stable category or that objects of homosexual love must disappear through the force of repudiation and prohibition? To what extent must we align this more general and inevitable separation and loss with a repudiation of homosexual love which makes gender melancholics of us all? The "givenness" of sexual difference is clearly not to be denied, and I agree that there is no "third sex" to be found or pursued. But why is sexual difference the primary *guarantor* of loss in our psychic lives? And can all separation and loss be traced back to that structuring loss of the other sex by which we emerge as this sexed being in the world?

Perhaps this assumption is troubled if we take seriously the notion that sex is at once given and accomplished—given as that which is (always) yet to be accomplished—and that it is accomplished in part through a heterosexualization of libidinal aims. This appeared to be Freud's argument in the opening chapters of *Three Essays on the Theory of Sexuality*. To what extent does the heterosexual frame for desire and loss cast the problem of separation and loss first and foremost as a problem of sexual difference?

Consider the following problematic, which is not quite in Phillips's language, but touches on the framework that he espouses. Does it follow that if one desires a woman, one is desiring from a masculine disposition, or is that disposition retroactively attributed to the desiring position as a way of retaining heterosexuality as the way of understanding the separateness or alterity that conditions desire? For if that claim were true, every woman who desires another woman desires her from a masculine disposition and is "heterosexual" to that degree; oddly, though, if the other woman desires her in return, the economy becomes one of male homosexuality(!). Does this theoretical frame not misunderstand the modes of alterity that persist within homosexuality, reducing the homosexual to a pursuit of sameness which is, in fact, very rarely the case (or is as often the case in heterosexual pursuit)?

Is this explanation through recourse to masculine disposition not an instance of the theoretical construction of "masculinity" or of the masculine "sex" which covers over—or forecloses—the possibility of another terminology which would avow a rich psychic world of attachment and loss which is not finally reducible to a given notion of sexual difference? Indeed, to what extent are our notions of the masculine and the feminine formed through the lost attachments which they are said to occasion? Can we finally ever resolve the question of whether sexual difference is the accomplishment of a melancholic heterosexuality, sacralized as theory, or whether it is the given condition of loss and attachment in any set of human relations? It seems clear that in some cases it is both, but that we would lose a vital terminology for understanding loss and its formative effects if we were to assume from the outset that we only and always lose the other sex, for it is as often the case that we are often in the melancholic bind of having lost our own sex in order, paradoxically, to become it.

Psychic Inceptions

Melancholy, Ambivalence, Rage

Conflicts between the ego and the ideal . . . ultimately reflect
the contrast between what is real and what is psychical,
between the external world and the internal world.
           —Freud, *The Ego and the Id*

In "Mourning and Melancholia," melancholy at first appears to be an aberrant form of mourning, in which one denies the loss of an object (an other or an ideal) and refuses the task of grief, understood as breaking attachment to the one who is lost. This lost object is magically retained as part of one's psychic life. The social world appears to be eclipsed in melancholy, and an internal world structured in ambivalence emerges as the consequence. It is not immediately clear how melancholy might be read, then, in terms of social life,[1] in particular, in terms of the social regulation of psychic life. Yet the account of melancholy is an account of how psychic and social domains are produced in relation to one another. As such, melancholy offers potential insight into how the boundaries of the social are instituted and maintained, not only at the expense of psychic life, but through binding psychic life into forms of melancholic ambivalence.

Melancholia thus returns us to the figure of the "turn" as a founding trope in the discourse of the psyche. In Hegel, turning back upon oneself comes to signify the ascetic and skeptical modes of reflexivity that mark the unhappy consciousness; in Nietzsche, turning back on oneself suggests a retracting of what one has said or done, or a recoiling in shame in the face of what one has done. In Althusser, the turn that the pedestrian makes toward the voice of the law is at once reflexive (the moment of becoming a subject whose self-consciousness is mediated by the law) and self-subjugating.

According to the narrative of melancholia that Freud provides, the ego is said to "turn back upon itself" once love fails to find its object and instead takes itself as not only an object of love, but of aggression and hate as well. But what is this "self" that takes itself as its own object? Is the one who "takes" itself and the one who is "taken" the same? This seduction of reflexivity seems to founder logically, since it is unclear that this ego can exist prior to its melancholia. The "turn" that marks the melancholic response to loss appears to initiate the redoubling of the ego as an object; only by turning back on itself does the ego acquire the status of a perceptual object. Moreover, the attachment to the object that is understood in melancholia to be redirected toward the ego undergoes a fundamental transformation in the course of that redirection. Not only is the attachment said to go from love to hate as it moves from the object to the ego, but the ego itself is produced as a *psychic object*; in fact, the very articulation of this psychic space, sometimes figured as "internal," depends on this melancholic turn.

The turn from the object to the ego produces the ego, which substitutes for the object lost. This production is a tropological

generation and follows from the psychic compulsion to substitute for objects lost. Thus, in melancholia not only does the
ego substitute for the object, but this act of substitution *institutes* the ego as a necessary response to or "defense" against
loss. To the extent that the ego is "the precipitate of its abandoned object-cathexes," it is the congealment of a history of
loss, the sedimentation of relations of substitution over time,
the resolution of a tropological function into the ontological
effect of the self.

Moreover, this substitution of ego for object does not quite
work. The ego is a poor substitute for the lost object, and its
failure to substitute in a way that satisfies (that is, to overcome
its status *as* a substitution), leads to the ambivalence that distinguishes melancholia. The turn from the object to the ego can
never quite be accomplished; it involves figuring the ego on
the model of the object (as suggested in the introductory paragraphs of "On Narcissism"); it also involves the unconscious
belief that the ego might compensate for the loss that is suffered. To the extent that the ego fails to provide such compensation, it exposes the faultlines in its own tenuous foundations.

Are we to accept that the ego turns from the object to the
ego, or that the ego turns its passion, as one might redirect a
wheel, from the object *to itself*? Does the same ego turn its investment from the object to itself, or is the ego fundamentally
altered by virtue of becoming the object of such a turn? What
is the status of "investment" and "attachment"? Do they indicate a free-floating desire that remains the same regardless of
the kind of object to which it is directed? Does the turn not
only produce the ego by which it is ostensibly initiated but
also structure the attachment it is said to redirect?

Is such a turn or redirection even possible? The loss for
which the turn seeks to compensate is not overcome, and the

object is not restored; rather, the loss becomes the opaque condition for the emergence of the ego, a loss that haunts it from the start as constitutive and avowable. Freud remarks that in mourning the object is "declared" lost or dead, but in melancholia, it follows, no such declaration is possible.[2] Melancholia is precisely the effect of unavowable loss. A loss prior to speech and declaration, it is the limiting condition of its possibility: a withdrawal or retraction from speech that makes speech possible. In this sense, melancholia makes mourning possible, a view that Freud came to accept in *The Ego and the Id*.

The inability to declare such a loss signifies the "retraction" or "absorption" of the loss by the ego. Clearly, the ego does not literally take an object inside itself, as if the ego were a kind of shelter prior to its melancholy. The psychological discourses that presume the topographical stability of an "internal world" and its various "parts" miss the crucial point that melancholy is precisely what interiorizes the psyche, that is, makes it possible to refer to the psyche through such topographical tropes. The turn from object to ego is the movement that makes the distinction between them possible, that marks the division, the separation or loss, that forms the ego to begin with. In this sense, the turn from the object to the ego fails successfully to substitute the latter for the former, but does succeed in marking and perpetuating the partition between the two. The turn thus produces the divide between ego and object, the internal and external worlds that it appears to presume.

If a preconstituted ego were able to make such a turn from an object to itself, it appears that it would have to turn from a preconstituted external reality to an internal one. But such an explanation could not account for the very division between internal and external on which it depends. Indeed, it is unclear that such a division can be understood apart from its context in melancholia. In what follows, I hope to clarify how melancholia involves the production of an internal world as well as a topographical set of fictions that structures the psyche. If the melancholic turn is the mechanism by which the distinction between internal and external worlds is instituted, then melancholia initiates a variable boundary between the psychic and the social, a boundary, I hope to show, that distributes and regulates the psychic sphere in relation to prevailing norms of social regulation.

That a love or desire or libidinal attachment is understood to take *itself* as its object, and to do this through the figure of the turn, suggests once again the tropological beginnings of subject formation. Freud's essay presumes that love of the object comes first, and only upon the loss of the object does melancholy emerge. Considered closely, however, Freud's essay makes clear that there can be no ego without melancholia, that the ego's loss is constitutive. The narrative grammar that might account for this relationship is necessarily confounded from the start.

Melancholia does not name a psychic process that might be recounted through an adequate explanatory scheme. It tends to confound any explanation of psychic process that we might be inclined to offer. And the reason it confounds any such effort is that it makes clear that our ability to refer to the psyche through tropes of internality are themselves effects of a melancholic condition. Melancholia produces a set of spatializing tropes for psychic life, domiciles of preservation and shelter as well as arenas for struggle and persecution. Such tropes do not "explain" melancholia: they constitute some of its fabular discursive effects.[3] In a manner that recalls Nietzsche's account of the fabrication of conscience, Freud offers a view of conscience as an agency and "institution" produced and maintained by melancholy.

Although Freud seeks to distinguish mourning and melancholia in this essay, he offers a portrait of melancholia that continually blurs into his view of mourning. He begins his description, for instance, by remarking that mourning may be a "reaction to the loss of a loved person, or to the loss of some abstraction that has taken the place of one, such as one's country, liberty, an ideal, and so on" (243). At first, mourning seems to have two forms, one in which someone is lost, someone real is lost, and another, in which what is lost in the someone real is ideal, the loss of an ideal. As the essay progresses, it appears that the loss of the ideal, "the loss of a more ideal kind" is correlated with melancholia. Already within mourning, however, the loss may be of an abstraction or an ideal, one that has taken the place of the one who is lost. A few paragraphs later, he notes that "melancholia too may be the reaction to the loss of a loved object" and that "where the exciting causes are different [from mourning] one can recognize that there is a loss of a more ideal kind." If one mourns for the loss of an ideal, and that ideal may substitute for a person who has been lost, or whose love is believed to be lost, then it makes no sense to claim that melancholia is distinguished as a loss of "a more ideal kind." And yet, a different kind of distinction between the two emerges when Freud claims, with reference to mourning, that the ideal may have substituted for the person and, with reference to melancholia, that the melancholic "knows whom he has lost but not *what* he has lost in him." In melancholia, the ideal that the person represents appears to be unknowable; in mourning, the person, or the ideal that substitutes for the person and that, presumably, renders the person lost, is unknowable.

Freud says melancholia is related to "an object-loss withdrawn from consciousness," but to the extent that mourning is related to substitute ideals and abstractions such as "country and liberty," it too is clearly constituted through the loss of the object, a double loss that involves both the substitute ideal and the person. Whereas in melancholia the ideal is occluded and one does not know what one has lost "in" the person lost, in mourning one risks not knowing whom one has lost "in" losing the ideal.

Later in the essay Freud specifies the psychic systems in which melancholy takes place and what it means for melancholy to be related to "an object-loss withdrawn from consciousness." He writes that "the unconscious [thing-]presentation [*Dingvorstellung*] of the object has been abandoned by the libido" (256).⁴ The "thing-presentation" of the object is not the object itself, but a cathected trace, one that is, in relation to the object, already a substitute and a derivative. In mourning, the traces of the object, its innumerable "links," are overcome piecemeal over time. In melancholia, the presence of ambivalence in relation to the object makes any such progressive de-linking of libidinal attachment impossible. Rather, "countless separate struggles are carried on over the object, in which love and hate contend with each other; the one seeks to detach the libido from the object, the other to maintain this position of the libido against the assault." This strange battlefield is to be found, Freud maintains, in "the region of the memory-traces of *things*."

Ambivalence may be a characteristic feature of every love attachment that a particular ego makes, or it may "proceed precisely from those experiences that involved the threat of losing the object" (256). This last remark suggests, however, that *ambivalence may well be a result of loss,* that the loss of an object precipitates an ambivalence toward it as part of the process of letting it go.[5] If so, then melancholia, defined as the ambivalent reaction to loss, may be coextensive with loss, so that mourning is subsumed in melancholia. Freud's statement that melancholia arises from "an object-loss withdrawn from consciousness" is thus specified in relation to ambivalence: "everything to do with these struggles due to ambivalence remains withdrawn from consciousness, until the outcome characteristic of melancholia has set in." The ambivalence remains *entzogen*—withdrawn—only to take on a specific form in melancholia, one in which different aspects of the psyche are accorded opposing positions within the relation of ambivalence. Freud offers this psychic articulation of ambivalence as "a conflict between one part of the ego and the critical agency" as an account of the formation of the super-ego in its critical relation to the ego. Ambivalence thus precedes the psychic topography of super-ego/ego; its melancholic articulation is offered as the condition of possibility of that very topography. Thus, it would make no sense to seek recourse to such a topography *to explain* melancholia, if the ambivalence that is said to distinguish melancholia is what then becomes articulated—after a period of being withdrawn from consciousness—as ego and super-ego. The internal topography by which melancholia is partially explained is itself the effect of that melancholia. Walter Benjamin remarks that melancholia spatializes, and that its effort to reverse or suspend time produces "landscapes" as its signature effect.[6] One might profitably read the Freudian topography that melancholy occasions as precisely such a spatialized landscape of the mind.

The ambivalence that is withdrawn from consciousness remains withdrawn "until the outcome characteristic of melancholy has set in" (257; "bis night der für die Melancholie charakteristische Ausgang eingetreten ist" [211]). What is this characteristic "exit" or "point of departure" that melancholy takes? Freud writes, "this, as we know, consists in the threatened libidinal cathexis at length abandoning the object, only, however, to draw back to the place in the ego from which it has proceeded." A more precise translation would clarify that melancholia involves an attempt to substitute the ego for that cathexis, one that involves a return of the cathexis to its point of origin: the threatened cathexis is abandoned, but only *to pull itself back onto the place of the ego* ("aber nur, um sich auf die Stelle des Ichs . . . zurückzuziehen"), a place from which the threatened attachment has departed ("von der sie ausgegangen war").

In melancholia, cathexis is understood to engage reflexively with itself ("um sich auf die Stelle des Ichs . . . zurückzuziehen") and, specifically, to draw or pull itself in and back to the place of its own departure or going-out. This "place" of the ego is not quite the same as the ego itself, but seems to represent a point of departure, an *Ausgangspunkt*, for the libido, as well as the melancholic site of its return. In this return of libido to its place of departure, a place of the ego, a melancholic circumscription of libido takes place.

This return is described as a withdrawal, a drawing or pulling back (*zurückziehung*), but also, in the next line, as a flight: "Die Liebe hat sich so durch ihre Flucht ins Ich der Aufhebung entzogen" (210).[7] Although this line is translated infamously as "So by taking flight into the ego love escapes extinction" (257), the sense of escaping extinction is not precisely right. The word *entzogen*, for instance, was previously translated as "withdrawn" and *Aufhebung* carries a notoriously ambiguous set of meanings from its circulation within Hegelian discourse: cancellation but not quite extinction; suspension, preservation, and overcoming. Through its flight into the ego, or in the ego, love has withdrawn or taken away its own overcoming, withdrawn a transformation, rendered it psychic. Here it is not a question of love "escaping an extinction" mandated from elsewhere; rather, love itself withdraws or takes away the destruction of the object, takes it on as its own destructiveness. Instead of breaking with the object, or transforming the object through mourning, this *Aufhebung*—this active, negating, and transformative movement—is taken into the ego. The "flight" of love into the ego is this effort to squirrel the *Aufhebung* away inside, to withdraw it from external reality, and to institute an internal topography in which the ambivalence might find an altered articulation. The withdrawal of ambivalence thus produces the possibility of a psychic transformation, indeed, a fabulation of psychic topography.

This flight and withdrawal is named, in the next line, as a regression, one that makes possible the conscious representation of melancholia: "After this regression of the libido the process can become conscious, *and it is represented to consciousness as a conflict between one part of the ego and the critical agency* [und repräsentiert sich dem Bewusstsein als ein Konflikt zwischen einem Teil des Ichs und der kritischen Instanz; my emphasis]."

Whereas one might expect that the regression of the libido, its being withdrawn into consciousness (as well as the withdrawal of ambivalence into consciousness) is the failure of its articulation, the opposite appears to be the case. Only upon the condition of such a withdrawal does melancholia take a conscious form. The withdrawal or regression of libido is represented to consciousness as a conflict between parts of the ego; indeed, the ego comes to be represented in parts only on the condition that such a withdrawal or regression has taken place. If melancholia constitutes the withdrawal or regression of ambivalence, and if that ambivalence becomes conscious through being represented as oppositional parts of the ego, and that representation is made possible on the condition of that withdrawal, then it follows that this prefiguration of the topographical distinction between ego and super-ego is itself dependent upon melancholia. Melancholia produces the possibility for the representation of psychic life. The *Aufhebung* that is withdrawn—one that might have meant the overcoming of loss through attachment to a substitute object—is an *Aufhebung* that reemerges within and as representation, a cancellation and preservation of the object, a set of "word-traces" (to use Freud's term) that becomes the psychoanalytic representation of psychic life.

To what extent does melancholia represent an otherwise unrepresentable ambivalence by fabulating psychic topographies? Representation is itself implicated in melancholia, that is, the effort to re-present that is at an infinite distance from its object. More specifically, melancholia provides the condition of possibility for the articulation of psychic topographies, of the ego in its constitutive relation to the super-ego and thus of the ego itself. Although the ego is said to be the point of departure for a libido that is subsequently withdrawn into the ego, it now appears that only upon such a withdrawal can the ego emerge as an object for consciousness, something that might be represented at all, whether as a point of departure or a site of return. Indeed, the phrase "withdrawn into the ego" is the retroactive product of the melancholic process it purports to describe. Thus it does not, strictly speaking, describe a pre-constituted psychic process but emerges in a belated fashion as a representation conditioned by melancholic withdrawal.

This last point raises the question of the status of the psychic topographies that predominate in this and other essays by Freud. Although one might expect that such topographies are to be read as the explanatory apparatus of psychoanalysis and not, as it were, one of its textualized symptoms, Freud suggests that the very distinction between ego and super-ego can be traced to an ambivalence that is first withdrawn from consciousness and then reemerges as a psychic topography in which "critical agency" is split off from the ego. Similarly, in his discussion of the self-beratements of the super-ego, he refers tellingly to conscience as "one of the major institutions of the ego."

Clearly playing on a metaphor of a socially constructed domain of power, Freud's reference to conscience as "among the major institutions of the ego [*Ichinstitutionen*]" (247) suggests not only that conscience is instituted, produced, and maintained within a larger polity and its organization, but that the ego and its various parts are accessible through a metaphorical language that attributes a social content and structure to these presumably psychic phenomena. Although Freud begins his essay by insisting on the indisputably "psychogenic nature" (243) of the melancholia and mourning under consideration in the essay, he also provides social metaphors that not only govern the topographic descriptions of melancholy's operation, but implicitly undo his own claim to provide a specifically psychogenic explanation of these psychic states. Freud describes "one part of the ego [that] sets itself over against the other, judges it critically, and, as it were, takes it as its object." A critical agency is said to be "split off" (*abgespalten*) from the ego, suggesting that in some prior state, this critical faculty was not yet separate. How, precisely, this splitting of the ego into parts occurs is, it seems, part of the strange, fabulating scene initiated by melancholy, the withdrawal of cathexis from the object to the ego, and the subsequent emergence of a representation of the psyche in terms of splits and parts, articulating ambivalence and internal antagonism. Is this topography not symptomatic of what it seeks to explain? How else do we explain this interiorization of the psyche and its expression here as a scene of partition and confrontation? Is there an implicit social text in this topographical rendition of psychic life, one that installs antagonism (the threat of judgment) as the structural necessity of the topographical model, one that follows from melancholia and from a withdrawal of attachment?

Melancholia describes a process by which an originally external object is lost, or an ideal is lost, and the refusal to break the attachment to such an object or ideal leads to the withdrawal of the object into the ego, the replacement of the object by the ego, and the setting up of an inner world in which a critical agency is split off from the ego and proceeds to take the ego as its object. In a well-known passage, Freud makes clear that the accusations that the critical agency is said to level against the ego turn out to be very much like the accusations that the ego would have leveled against the object or the ideal. Thus, the ego absorbs both love and rage against the object. Melancholia appears to be a process of internalization, and one might well read its effects as a psychic state that has effectively substituted itself for the world in which it dwells. The effect of melancholia, then, appears to be the loss of the social world, the substitution of psychic parts and antagonisms for external relations among social actors: "an object-loss was transformed into an ego-loss and the conflict between the ego and the loved person into a cleavage between the critical activity of the ego and the ego as altered by identification" (249).

The object is lost, and the ego is said to withdraw the object into itself. The "object" thus withdrawn is already magical, a trace of some kind, a representative of the object, but not the object itself, which is, after all, gone. The ego into which this remnant is "brought" is not exactly a shelter for lost part-objects, although it is sometimes described that way. The ego is "altered by identification," that is, altered by virtue of absorbing the object or pulling back its own cathexis onto itself. The "price" of such an identification, however, is that the ego splits into the critical agency and the ego as object of criticism and judgment. Thus the relation to the object reappears "in" the ego, not merely as a mental event or singular representation, but as a scene of self-beratement that reconfigures the topography of the ego, a fantasy of internal partition and judgment that comes to structure the representation of psychic life *tout court*. The ego now stands for the object, and the critical agency comes to represent the ego's disowned rage, reified as a psychic agency separate from the ego itself. That rage, and the attachment it implies, are "turned back upon" the ego, but from where?

Yet certain socially identifiable features of the melancholic, including "communicativeness," suggest that melancholia is not an asocial psychic state. In fact, melancholia is produced to the extent that the social world is eclipsed by the psychic, that a certain transfer of attachment from objects to ego takes place, not without a contamination of the psychic sphere by the social sphere that is abandoned. Freud suggests as much when he explains that the lost other is not simply brought inside the ego, as one might shelter a wayward dog. The act of internalization (to be construed as a fantasy rather than as a process[8]) transforms the object (one might even use the term *Aufhebung* for such a transformation); the other is taken in and transformed into an ego, but an ego to be reviled, thereby both producing and strengthening the critical "agency . . . commonly called conscience." A form of moral reflexivity is produced in which the ego splits itself to furnish an internal perspective by which to judge itself. This reflexive relation by which the ego becomes an object for itself turns out to be a withdrawn and transformed (*entzogen* and *aufgehoben*) relation to the lost other; in this sense, reflexivity appears to depend upon the prior operation of melancholia. The ego is also figured as having a *voice* through this process, and it appears imperative within melancholia that self-beratement be voiced, not merely to oneself, but in the presence of others. The self-reproaches of the ego are not simply the imitation of reproaches once leveled against the ego from the one lost, as is commonly assumed; rather, they are reproaches leveled against the other that now turn back upon the ego.

Before we consider more closely what it means for something to "turn back upon itself" in this way, it seems important to note that the psychic form of reflexivity melancholia elaborates carries the trace of the other within it as a dissimulated sociality, and that the performance of melancholia as the shameless voicing of self-beratement in front of others effects a detour that rejoins melancholia to its lost or withdrawn sociality. In melancholia, not only is the loss of an other or an ideal lost to consciousness, but the social world in which such a loss became possible is also lost. The melancholic does not merely withdraw the lost object from consciousness, but withdraws into the psyche a configuration of the social world as well. The ego thus becomes a "polity" and conscience one of its "major institutions," precisely because psychic life withdraws a social world into itself in an effort to annul the losses that world demands. Within melancholia, the psyche becomes the topos in which there is no loss and, indeed, no negation. Melancholia refuses to acknowledge loss, and in this sense "preserves" its lost objects as psychic effects.

Freud remarks the social conduct of the melancholic, emphasizing his or her shameless self-exposure: "the melancholic does not behave in quite the same way as a person who is crushed by remorse and self-reproach in a normal fashion. Feelings of shame are lacking . . . or . . . are not prominent. . . . One might emphasize the presence in him of an almost opposite trait of insistent communicativeness which finds satisfaction in self-exposure" (247). The melancholic sustains an indirect and deflected relationship to the sociality from which he or she has withdrawn. One *would have* denounced the lost other if one could—for departing, if for no other reason. Fulfilling a wish whose form, the past subjunctive, precludes any such fulfillment, the melancholic seeks not only to reverse time, reinstating the imaginary past as the present, but to occupy every position and thereby to preclude the loss of the addressee. The melancholic would have *said something*, if he or she could, but did not, and now believes in the sustaining power of the voice. Vainly, the melancholic now says what he or she would have said, addressed only to himself, as one who is already split off from himself, but whose power of self-address depends upon this self-forfeiture. The melancholic thus burrows in a direction opposite to that in which he might find a fresher trace of the lost other, attempting to resolve the loss through psychic substitutions and compounding the loss as he goes. A failure of address, a failure to sustain the other through the voice that addresses, melancholia emerges as a compensatory form of negative narcissism: I revile myself and rehabilitate the other in the form of my own internal ambivalence. I refuse to speak to or of the other, but I speak voluminously about myself, leaving a refracted trail of what I did not say to or about the other. The stronger the inhibition against expression, the stronger the expression of conscience.

How does this problem of the unconscious loss, the refused loss, that marks melancholia return us to the problem of the relation between the psychic and the social? In mourning, Freud tells us, there is nothing about the loss that is unconscious. In melancholia, he maintains, "the object-loss is withdrawn from consciousness": the object is not only lost, but that loss itself is lost, withdrawn and preserved in the suspended time of psychic life. In other words, according to the melancholic, "I have lost nothing."

The unspeakability and unrepresentability of this loss translates directly into a heightening of conscience. Where one might expect that conscience would wax and wane according to the strength of externally imposed prohibitions, it appears that its strength has more to do with marshalling aggression in the service of refusing to acknowledge a loss that has already taken place, a refusal to lose a time that is already gone. Oddly, the psyche's moralism appears to be an index of its own thwarted grief and illegible rage. Thus, if the relation between melancholia and social life is to be reestablished, it is not to be measured by regarding the self-beratements of conscience as mimetic internalizations of the beratements leveled by social agencies of judgment or prohibition. Rather, forms of social power emerge that regulate what losses will and will not be grieved; in the social foreclosure of grief we might find what fuels the internal violence of conscience.

Although social power regulates what losses can be grieved, it is not always as effective as it aims to be. The loss cannot fully be denied, but neither does it appear in a way that can directly be affirmed. The "plaints" of the melancholic are invariably misdirected, yet in this misdirection resides a nascent political text. The prohibition on grief registers as a loss of speech for its addressee. The pain of loss is "credited" to the one who suffers it, at which point the loss is understood as a fault or injury deserving of redress; one seeks redress for harms done to oneself, but from no one except oneself.

The violence of social regulation is not to be found in its unilateral action, but in the circuitous route by which the psyche accuses itself of its own worthlessness. No doubt, this is a strange and opaque symptom of unresolved grief. Why does the retraction of the lost other into the ego, the refusal to acknowledge loss, culminate in a deprivation of the ego? Is the loss resituated in a way that nullifies the ego in order, psychically, to save the object? The decrease in self-esteem that is said to distinguish melancholia from mourning appears to result from prodigious efforts by the critical agency to deprive the ego of its esteem. But one could equally say that there is no question of high or low self-esteem prior to the operation of this critical agency, no "esteem" that belongs to the ego prior to its partition into ego and super-ego. Prior to the operation of a critical agency, it would be difficult to gauge the ego against an ideal, a judgment that presupposes a critical agency that might approve or disapprove of the ego's moral state. In this sense, self-esteem appears to be produced by the very critical agency by which it is potentially destroyed.

Freud does refer to this resituating of loss in the ego when he refers to the ego as impoverished, as having become poor, and "an object-loss . . . transformed into an ego-loss" (249). This loss in the ego is apparently a loss of an ideal of itself, and in Freud's later work, he specifies that the judgments of conscience work in such a way that the super-ego gauges the ego against the "ego-ideal." The ego is found to be impoverished beside this ideal, and the "loss" that the ego suffers is a loss of commensurability between itself and the ideal by which it is judged. Where does this ideal emerge from? Is it arbitrarily manufactured by the ego, or do such ideals retain the trace of social regulation and normativity? Freud remarks that melancholia is a response not just to death, but to other orders of loss, including "slights and disappointments" (250). And when he introduces the notion that both mourning and melancholia can be responses to the loss of an ideal, such as "country" or "liberty," he makes clear by his examples that such ideals are social in character.

The ideals by which the ego judges itself clearly are ones by which the ego will be found wanting. The melancholic compares him- or herself invidiously with such social ideals. If they are the psychic sanctification of once-external objects or ideals, then they are seemingly also the target of aggression. Indeed, we might well ask whether the situation in which the ego is, as it were, berated by the ideal is not the inversion of a prior situation in which the ego would, if it could, have berated the ideal. Is the psychic violence of conscience not a refracted indictment of the social forms that have made certain kinds of losses ungrievable?

Thus, a loss in the world that cannot be declared enrages, generates ambivalence, and becomes the loss "in" the ego that is nameless and diffuse and that prompts public rituals of self-beratement. Of mourning, Freud writes that it "impels the ego to give up the object by *declaring* the object to be dead" (257, my emphasis). Melancholia, it would follow, refuses to make any such declaration, declines speech, suspending the "verdict of reality that the object no longer exists" (255). We know, however, that the melancholic is also "communicative," which suggests that his or her speech is neither verdictive nor declarative (assertoric), but inevitably indirect and circuitous. What cannot be declared by the melancholic is nevertheless what governs melancholic speech—an unspeakability that organizes the field of the speakable.

"The loss of the melancholic seems puzzling to us because *we cannot see what it is* that is absorbing him so entirely" (247). What cannot be directly spoken is also what is occluded from sight, absent from the visual field that organized melancholia. Melancholia is kept from view; it is an absorption by something that cannot be accommodated by vision, that resists being brought into the open, neither seen nor declared. As private and irrecoverable as this loss seems, the melancholic is strangely outgoing, pursuing an "insistent communicativeness which finds satisfaction in self-exposure" (247). The worthlessness of the ego is insistently communicated. Melancholic speech, neither verdictive nor declarative, remains unable to speak its loss. What the melancholic does declare, namely, his own worthlessness, identifies the loss at the sight of the ego and, hence, continues to fail to identify the loss. Self-beratement takes the place of abandonment, and becomes the token of its refusal.

The heightening of conscience under such circumstances attests to the unavowed status of the loss. The ego becomes moralized on the condition of ungrieved loss. But what conditions make it possible to grieve, or not to grieve, loss?

The ego not only brings the object inside but brings aggression against the object along with it. The more this object is brought inside, as it were, the higher the self-debasement, the poorer the ego becomes: delusional self-abasement "overcomes the instinct which compels every living thing to life"

(246). The aggression turned against the ego has the power to contest and overcome the desire to live. At this point in Freud's theory, aggression against oneself is derived from an outwardly directed aggression against an other. But one can discern in this formulation the beginnings of reflection on a drive that might be said to counter the pleasure principle, what is later referred to as the death drive.

In melancholia, the ego contracts something of the loss or abandonment by which the object is now marked, an abandonment that is refused and, as refused, is incorporated. In this sense, to refuse a loss is to become it. If the ego cannot accept the loss of the other, then the loss that the other comes to represent becomes the loss that now characterizes the ego: the ego becomes poor and impoverished. A loss suffered in the world becomes now the characteristic lack in the ego (a split that is, as it were, imported through the necessary work of internalization).

In this way, melancholia operates in a direction directly counter to narcissism. Echoing the biblical cadence of "the shadow of death," a way in which death imposes its presence on life, Freud remarks that in melancholia "the shadow of the object fell upon the ego" (249). In Lacan's essays on narcissism, the formulation is importantly reversed: the shadow of the ego falls upon the object.[9] Narcissism continues to control love, even when that narcissism appears to give way to object-love: it is still myself that I find there at the site of the object, my absence. In melancholia this formulation is reversed: in the place of the loss that the other comes to represent, I find myself to be that loss, impoverished, wanting. In narcissistic love, the other contracts my abundance. In melancholia, I contract the other's absence.

This opposition between melancholia and narcissism gestures toward the dual-drive theory. Freud is clear that melancholia must be understood in part as a narcissistic disturbance. Some of its features come from narcissism, but some come from mourning. In making this claim, Freud appears to set mourning as a limit to narcissism, or perhaps, as its counter-direction. What erodes the ego in melancholia is understood to be a loss that was originally external, but by *The Ego and the Id* Freud comes to recognize that the work of melancholia may well be in the service of the death drive. He asks, "How is it then that in melancholia the super-ego can become a gathering-place for the death instincts?"[10] How is it that the ego-eroding effects of melancholia, the ones that overcome "the instinct which compels every living thing to life," come to work in the service of a drive that seeks to overcome life? Freud goes further and remarks that the "merciless violence" of conscience shows that "what is now holding sway in the super-ego is, as it were, a pure culture of the death instinct [*Todestrieb*]" (53). In melancholia, then, according to this revised theory published in *The Ego and the Id*, it would be impossible to separate the death drive from the conscience heightened through melancholia. In either case, the ego risks its life in the face of its failure to live up to the standards encoded in the ego-ideal. And the aggression it takes upon itself is in part proportional to the aggression against the other that it has managed to bring under control.

In this account of melancholia, reflexivity emerges, as it does for Nietzsche, as a transposed aggressivity. As we have seen, for Freud in "Mourning and Melancholia," aggression is primarily a relation to others and only secondarily a relation to oneself. He remarks that the suicidal person must first have undergone murderous impulses, and suggests that self-torment satisfies sadism and hate. Both of these impulses have been experienced as "turned around upon the subject's own self" (251) — "eine Wendung gegen die eigene Person erfahren haben." The ambivalence that contains this aggression splits the cathexis, which is then distributed into "parts": part of the erotic cathexis regresses to identification; the other part to sadism. Set up as internal parts of the ego, the sadistic part takes aim at the part that identifies, and the psychically violent drama of the super-ego proceeds. Freud appears to assume ambivalence at the scene of loss: a wish for the other to die or to go (a wish that is sometimes instigated by the desire of the ego to live and, hence, break its attachment to what has gone or died). Freud interprets this ambivalence as at once an instance of sadism and a wish to preserve the other as oneself. Self-torment is this sadism turned back on the ego, encoding and dissimulating the dual desire to vanquish and to save the object. Self-punishment, he notes, is "the circuitous path" of sadism; we might add, it is the circuitous path of identification as well.

Freud appears clear here that sadism precedes masochism. (His later emphasis on the death drive will invert this priority.) Reflexive articulations of aggression are always derived from outwardly directed ones. We have known for some time, he writes, that "no neurotic harbors thoughts of suicide which he has not turned back upon himself [*auf sich zurückwendet*] from murderous impulses toward others" (252). The ego takes itself as an object in the place of taking the other as an object. Indeed, the ego *first* takes itself as an object on the condition that it has *already* taken the other as an object, and that the other becomes the model by which the ego assumes its boundary as an object for itself — a kind of mimesis, not unlike that described by Mikkel Borch-Jacobsen,[11] in which mimetic activity produces the ego as an object on the model of the other. Mimesis within melancholia performs this activity as the incorporation of the other "into the ego." This is an effort to preserve the other and at the same time to dissimulate aggression toward the other.

Clearly, no Freudian theory that takes the ego as primary or pregiven can account for the way in which the ego first becomes an object on the condition of the internalization of aggression and the refusal of loss. Melancholia establishes the tenuous basis of the ego, and indicates something of its status as an instrument of *containment*. The significance of the ego as containing aggression becomes clear when we consider Freud's explicitly social metaphorics in these descriptions. One passage, noted by Homi Bhabha,[12] suggests something of the political analogy at issue. "Melancholic . . . reaction . . . proceeds from a mental constellation of revolt [*seelischen Konstellation der Auflehnung*], which has then, by a certain process, passed over into the crushed state of melancholia [*die melancholische Zerknirschung*]" (248).

Bhabha argues that melancholia is not a form of passivity, but a form of revolt that takes place through repetition and metonymy. The melancholic inverts against itself the indictment it would level against the other; this "incorporation" of the other is also, Bhabha notes, a "disincorporation of the Master." Underscoring that "the Law is entombed as loss at the point of its ideal authority," he argues that melancholia contests the ideality of that authority precisely by incorporating it.[13] Authority's ideality is incorporable elsewhere, no longer tied in any absolute sense to one figure of the law.

Melancholia is a rebellion that has been put down, crushed. Yet it is not a static affair; it continues as a kind of "work" that takes place by deflection. Figured within the workings of the psyche is the power of the state to preempt an insurrectionary rage. The "critical agency" of the melancholic is at once a social and psychic instrument. This super-egoic conscience is not simply analogous to the state's military power over its citizenry; the state cultivates melancholia among its citizenry precisely as a way of dissimulating and displacing its own ideal authority. This is not to suggest that conscience is a simple instantiation of the state; on the contrary, it is the vanishing point of the state's authority, its psychic idealization, and, in that sense, its disappearance as an external object. The process of forming the subject is a process of rendering the terrorizing power of the state invisible—and effective—as the ideality of conscience. Furthermore, the incorporation of the ideal of "Law" underscores the contingent relation between a given state and the ideality of its power. This ideality can always be incorporated elsewhere and remains incommensurable with any of its given incorporations. That this ideality cannot be reduced to any of its incorporations does not mean, however, that it subsists in a noumenal sphere beyond all embodiments. Rather, the incorporations are sites of rearticulation, conditions for a "working through" and, potentially, a "throwing off" (*Auflehnung*).

The revolt in melancholia can be distilled by marshalling aggression in the service of mourning, but also, necessarily, of life. As an instrument of psychic terror, conscience wields the power of condemnation that, quite literally, poses a threat to one's life. Freud notes that it "often enough succeeds in driving the ego into death, if the latter does not *fend off its tyrant* in time by the change round into mania."[14] Mania appears to be the energetic throwing off of the attachment to the lost object, enshrined in the workings of conscience. Yet in mania, "what the ego has surmounted and what it is triumphing over remain hidden from it."[15] In mania, the tyrant is fended off, but not thrown off or overcome. Mania marks a temporary suspension or mastering of the tyrant by the ego, but the tyrant remains structurally ensconced for that psyche—and unknowable. For a resolution of melancholia that is more thorough than any mania can provide, Freud suggests that "a verdict of reality" must be accepted for melancholia to become mourning, and for the attachment to the lost object to be severed. Indeed, the aggression instrumentalized by conscience against the ego is precisely what must be reappropriated in the service of the desire to live: "the libido's attachment to the lost object is met by the verdict of reality that the object no longer exists; and the ego, confronted as it were with the question whether it shall share this fate, is persuaded by the sum of the narcissistic satisfactions it derives from being alive to sever its attachment to the object that has been abolished" (255).

For the melancholic, breaking the attachment constitutes a second loss of the object. If the object lost its externality when it became a psychic ideal, it now loses its ideality as the ego turns against conscience, thus decentering itself. The judgments of conscience are exchanged for the verdict of reality, and this verdict poses a dilemma for the melancholic, namely, whether to follow the lost object into death or to seize the opportunity to live. Later, Freud remarks that there can be no severing of this attachment to the object without a direct "declaration" of loss and the desanctification of the object by externalizing aggression against it: "Just as mourning impels the ego to give up the object by declaring the object to be dead and offering the ego the inducement to live, so does each single struggle of ambivalence loosen the fixation of the libido to the object by disparaging it, denigrating it and even as it were killing it off [*entwertet, herabsetzt, gleichsam auch erschlägt*]" (257). "Killing off" the critical agency reverses and displaces the interiorized scene of conscience and clears the way for psychic survival. Whereas melancholia involves a "delusional self-abasement . . . that overcomes the instinct which compels every living thing to life," the break with melancholia involves turning against the already "turned back" aggression that constitutes conscience. Survival, not precisely the opposite of melancholia, but what melancholia puts in suspension—requires redirecting rage against the lost other, defiling the sanctity of the dead for the purposes of life, raging against the dead in order not to join them.

Although such rage may be required to break the melancholic bind, there is no final reprieve from the ambivalence and no final separation of mourning from melancholia. Freud's view that mourning and melancholia might be distinguished is challenged not only in his own essay by that name, but explicitly in *The Ego and the Id*. Ambivalence, which is first identified as a possible response to loss in "Mourning and Melancholia," becomes, toward the end of the essay, the struggle that loss occasions between the desire to live and the desire to die. As such, both ambivalence and the struggle of life and death, to borrow Hegelian parlance, are occasioned by loss, indeed, instigated by loss. If ambivalence distinguishes melancholia from mourning, and if mourning entails ambivalence as part of the process of "working through," then there is no work of mourning that does not engage melancholia. As was remarked in the previous chapter, Freud argues in *The Ego and the Id* that the ego is composed of its lost attachments and that there would be no ego were there no internalization of loss along melancholic lines. The inverse of this position, however, is not pursued by Freud, although his theory points the way: if the ego contains aggression against the other who is gone, then it follows that reexternalizing that aggression "uncontains" the ego. The desire to live is not the desire of the ego, but a desire that undoes the ego in the course of its emergence. The "mastery" of the ego would then be identified as the effect of the death drive, and life, in a Nietzschean sense, would break apart that mastery, initiating a lived mode of becoming that contests the stasis and defensive status of the ego.

But the story of mourning cannot be reduced to one in which life triumphs over death. The dynamic is more complicated. Although in 1917 Freud does not yet distinguish between the pleasure principle and the death drive, he does note that melancholy has the power to force the ego into death. By 1923, he explicitly claims that conscience, as it functions in melancholia, is "a gathering place" for the death drives. In mourning, the claim of life does not triumph over the lure of death; on the contrary, the "death drives" are marshalled in the service of breaking with the object, "killing" the object in order to live. Further, insofar as the object resides as the ideality of conscience, and the ego is situated within that topographical scene, both conscience and the ego are necessarily undone by that murderous claim on life. The "death drive" is thus paradoxically necessary for survival; in mourning, the breaking of attachment inaugurates life. But this "break" is never final or full. One does not retract a quantity of libido from one object in order to invest it in another. To the extent that melancholy establishes the positionality of the ego, the distinction between the psychic and the social, it also functions to make possible an epistemological encounter with alterity. The conclusion of grief may undo the ego (in the sense of "unbinding" it from its cathexis in conscience), but it does not destroy it. There is no break with the constitutive historicity of loss to which melancholy attests (except perhaps in the manic response, which is always temporary). The historicity of loss is to be found in identification and, hence, in the very forms that attachment is bound to take. "Libido" and "attachment" in such a view could not be conceived as free-floating energies, but as having a historicity that could never fully be recovered.

If in "Mourning and Melancholia," Freud thought that one must sever one attachment to make another, in *The Ego and the Id*, he is clear that only upon the condition that the lost other becomes internalized can mourning ever be accomplished and new attachments begun. Here, of course, an unexplored point deserves remark: internalization does not have to take the form of a mercilessly violent conscience, and certain kinds of internalization, which are not always incorporations, are necessary for survival.[16] Indeed, Derrida insists, with the later Freud, that "mourning is the affirmative incorporation of the Other" and that, in principle, there can be no end to mourning.[17]

Indeed, one may rage against one's attachment to some others (which is simply to alter the terms of the attachment), but no rage can sever the attachment to alterity, except perhaps a suicidal rage that usually still leaves behind a note, a final address, thus confirming that allocutory bond. Survival does not take place because an autonomous ego exercises autonomy in confrontation with a countervailing world; on the contrary, no ego can emerge except through animating reference to such a world. Survival is a matter of avowing the trace of loss that inaugurates one's own emergence. To make of melancholia a simple "refusal" to grieve its losses conjures a subject who might already be something without its losses, that is, one who voluntarily extends and retracts his or her will. Yet the subject who might grieve is implicated in a loss of autonomy that is mandated by linguistic and social life; it can never produce itself autonomously. From the start, this ego is other than itself; what melancholia shows is that only by absorbing the other as oneself does one become something at all. The social terms which make survival possible, which interpellate social existence, never reflect the autonomy of the one who comes to recognize him- or herself in them and, thus, stands a chance "to be" within language. Indeed, by forfeiting that notion of autonomy survival becomes possible; the "ego" is released from its melancholic foreclosure of the social. The ego comes into being on the condition of the "trace" of the other, who is, at that moment of emergence, already at a distance. To accept the autonomy of the ego is to forget that trace; and to accept that trace is to embark upon a process of mourning that can never be complete, for no final severance could take place without dissolving the ego.

This insight that melancholia offers into the power of the trace of alterity to produce the ego "along a fictional line," as Lacan has put it, is not restricted to the trace of some specific set of others, that is, to the child and its mother or to other dyadic pairs. Indeed, the "other" may be an ideal, a country, a concept of liberty, in which the loss of such ideals is compensated by the interiorized ideality of conscience. An other or an ideal may be "lost" by being rendered unspeakable, that is, lost through prohibition or foreclosure: unspeakable, impossible to declare, but emerging in the indirection of complaint and the heightened judgments of conscience. Contained within the psychic topography of ambivalence, the faded social text requires a different sort of genealogy in the formation of the subject, one which takes into account how what remains unspeakably absent inhabits the psychic voice of the one who remains. The violence of the loss is redoubled and refracted in a violence of the psychic agency that threatens death; the social is "turned back" into the psychic, only to leave its trace in the voice of conscience. Conscience thus fails to instantiate social regulation; rather, it is the instrument of its dissimulation. To claim life in such circumstances is to contest the righteous psyche, not by an act of will, but by submission to a sociality and linguistic life that makes such acts possible, one that exceeds the bounds of the ego and its "autonomy." To persist in one's being means to be given over from the start to social terms that are never fully one's own. Those terms institute a linguistic life for the "one" who speaks prior to any act of agency, and they remain both irreducible to the one who speaks and the necessary conditions of such speech. In this sense, interpellation works by failing, that is, it institutes its subject as an agent precisely to the extent that it fails to determine such a subject exhaustively in time.

The inaugurative scene of interpellation is one in which a certain failure to be constituted becomes the condition of possibility for constituting oneself. Social discourse wields the power to form and regulate a subject through the imposition of its own terms. Those terms, however, are not simply accepted or internalized; they become psychic only through the movement by which they are dissimulated and "turned." In the absence of explicit regulation, the subject emerges as one for whom power has become voice, and voice, the regulatory instrument of the psyche. The speech acts of power—the declaration of guilt, the judgment of worthlessness, the verdicts of reality—are topographically rendered as psychic instruments and institutions within a psychic landscape that depends on its metaphoricity for its plausibility. Regulatory power becomes "internal" only through the melancholic production of the figure of internal space, one that follows from the withdrawing of resources—a withdrawal and turning of language, as well. By withdrawing its own presence, power becomes an object lost—"a loss of a more ideal kind." Eligible for melancholic incorporation, power no longer acts unilaterally on its subject. Rather, the subject is produced, paradoxically, through this withdrawal of power, its dissimulation and fabulation of the psyche as a speaking topos. Social power vanishes, becoming the object lost, or social power makes vanish, effecting a mandatory set of losses. Thus, it effects a melancholia that reproduces power as the psychic voice of judgment addressed to (turned upon) oneself, thus modeling reflexivity on subjection.

Some psychoanalytic theorists of the social have argued that social interpellation always produces a psychic excess it cannot control. Yet the production of the psychic as a distinct domain cannot obliterate the social occasion of this production. The "institution" of the ego cannot fully overcome its social residue, given that its "voice" is from the start borrowed from elsewhere, a recasting of a social "plaint" as psychic self-judgment.

The power imposed upon one is the power that animates one's emergence, and there appears to be no escaping this ambivalence. Indeed, there appears to be no "one" without ambivalence, which is to say that the fictive redoubling necessary to become a self rules out the possibility of strict identity. Finally, then, there is no ambivalence without loss as the verdict of sociality, one that leaves the trace of its turn at the scene of one's emergence.

Reference Matter

Notes

INTRODUCTION

1. Hayden White remarks in *Tropics of Discourse* (Baltimore: Johns Hopkins University Press, 1978) that "the word *tropic* derives from *tropikos, tropos,* which in classical Greek meant 'turn' and in Koiné 'way' or 'manner.' It comes into modern Indo-European languages by way of *tropus,* which in Classical Latin meant 'metaphor' or 'figure of speech' and in Late Latin, especially as applied to music theory, 'mood' or 'measure' " (p. 2). White goes on to associate the notion of trope with style, a term that he understands to distinguish the study of discourse from both the study of fiction and logic. Tropes are "deviations" from customary language, but they also generate figures of speech or thought (a distinction crucial to Quintillian's account as well). In this sense, a trope can produce a connection between terms that is not considered either customary or logical. For our purposes, this means that a trope operates in a way that is not restricted to accepted versions of reality. At the same time, a trope cannot operate, that is, generate new meanings or connections, if its departure from custom and logic is not recognized as such a departure. In this sense, a trope presupposes an accepted version of reality for its operation.

For Nietzsche, however, the recirculation and sedimentation of tropes is the condition of possibility for the customary use of language. Indeed, he argues that tropes are the stuff out of which literal and conceptual language emerges. Only through a kind of forgetfulness of the tropological status of language does something like customary language take hold. Customary language is the sedimentation or "deadening" effect of tropes. This suggestion is made clear, both argumentatively and rhetorically, in his essay "On Truth and Lie in an Extra-Moral Sense," in Friedrich Nietzsche, *On Rhetoric and Language*, ed. Sander Gilman et al. (New York: Oxford University Press, 1989).

"Turn" was an English term for "trope" in the seventeenth and eighteenth centuries, used in referring to several syntactical figures of speech. Richard Lanham writes that a trope is a specific kind of figure, one which changes the meaning of a word (*A Handlist of Rhetorical Terms*, Berkeley: University of California Press, 1991). Some argue for retaining the term "figure" for terms that change the meaning of more than one word. Quintillian objects to this distinction, insisting that this change of meaning happens in ways that are not reducible to single or plural words, and then defines a trope as a change of meaning, whereas "figure" is used for a change in form (i.e., the form of a pattern of speech or even a genre of writing). That this turn is considered generative or productive seems especially relevant to our consideration of the production or generation of the subject. Not only is generation what a trope does, but the explanation of generation seems to require the use of tropes, an operation of language that both reflects and enacts the generativity it seeks to explain, irreducibly mimetic and performative.

2. My discussion of "attachment" is indebted to Wendy Brown's essay "Wounded Attachments," in her *States of Injury: Freedom and Power in Late Modernity* (Princeton: Princeton University Press, 1995).

3. In "On Narcissism," Freud distinguishes between narcissistic and anaclitic forms of love, arguing that the former enhance or inflate the ego, and the latter lead to its diminution or impoverishment.

4. On the notion that repetition, signifying the death drive, marks the limit of the ego's mastery, see Jacques Lacan, *Four Fundamental Concepts of Psychoanalysis*, ed. J.-A. Miller, trans. Alan Sheridan (New York: Norton, 1978), pp. 40–49. Freud makes the argument in *Beyond the Pleasure Principle* (*The Standard Edition of the Complete Psychological Works of Sigmund Freud*, ed. and trans. James Strachey, 24 vols. [London: Hogarth, 1953–74], 18: 20–23).

5. This discussion continues arguments that I made in *Bodies That Matter: On the Discursive Limits of "Sex"* (New York: Routledge, 1993): "There is no power that acts, but only a reiterated acting that is power

in its persistence and instability" (p. 9). This statement was not meant to suggest that power acts without the subject. On the contrary, for power to act, there *must* be a subject, but that necessity does not make the subject into the origin of power.

6. Michel Foucault, *Discipline and Punish: The Birth of the Prison* (New York: Pantheon, 1977), *Surveiller et punir: Naissance de la prison* (Paris: Gallimard, 1975); *The History of Sexuality, Volume 1: An Introduction*, trans. Robert Hurley (New York: Vintage, 1978), *Histoire de la sexualité 1: Volonté de savoir* (Paris: Gallimard, 1978); *The Use of Pleasure: Volume 2 of The History of Sexuality* (New York: Pantheon, 1985), *L'usage des plaisirs*, (Paris: Gallimard, 1984); "Two Lectures," *Power/Knowledge: Selected Interviews and Other Writings, 1972–77*, ed. Colin Gordon (New York: Pantheon, 1980), pp. 78–108.

7. Lacan refers to the subject as excrescence.

8. Nietzsche develops the notion of the sign-chain (*Zeichenkette*) in *On the Genealogy of Morals*, trans. Walter Kaufmann (New York: Random House, 1967), pp. 77–78; *Zur Genealogie der Moral*, in Nietzsche, *Sämtliche Werke: Kritische Studienausgabe in 15 Einzelbänden*, ed. Giorgio Colli and Mazzino Montinari, vol. 5 (Berlin: de Gruyter, 1988), pp. 314–15. He remarks that the origin of a word or an instrument may come to assume purposes and produce effects for which it was never originally intended or fashioned.

9. I distinguish between internal and interior, according to conventions within phenomenology: "internal" designates a contingent relation; "interior," a constitutive relation. This terminology also underscores the phenomenological register of the latter.

10. Both authors use the word *Trieb* for drive. In addition, both figure this drive as what can and does turn back upon itself.

11. See Chapter 5 for a more detailed examination of this notion.

12. For a discussion of the lack of originary violence in Foucauldian notions of discursive productivity, see Gayatri Chakravorty Spivak's provocative essay "More on Power/Knowledge," in her *Outside in the Teaching Machine* (New York: Routledge, 1993), p. 33.

13. Freud's reflections on "Mourning and Melancholia" in *The Ego and the Id* become important for Melanie Klein's observations on incorporation.

14. Spinoza argues that "everything insofar as it is in itself, en-

deavors to persist in its own being" (p. 135), even as he insists that "a thing, which is conditioned to act in a particular manner, has necessarily been conditioned by God" (p. 61). Autonomy is thus always conditioned and, to that extent, subverted by the conditions of its own possibility. ("The Ethics," *Philosophy of Spinoza*, trans. R. H. M. Elwes [New York: Tudor Publishing House], 1934.)

CHAPTER 1

NOTE: This chapter originally appeared in David Clarke and Tilottama Rajan, eds., *Intersections: Nineteenth-Century Philosophy and Contemporary Theory* (Buffalo: SUNY Press, 1995). I would like to thank William Connolly and Peter Fenves for comments on earlier versions of this essay.

1. In the following text I refer to this chapter in abbreviated form as "The Unhappy Consciousness." English citations are from *The Phenomenology of Spirit*, trans. A. V. Miller (Oxford: Oxford University Press, 1977); German citations are from G. W. F. Hegel, *Werke in zwanzig Bänden*, vol. 3 (Frankfurt am Main: Suhrkamp, 1980). Page numbers for later citations will appear in the text.

2. Michel Foucault, *Discipline and Punish: The Birth of the Prison* (New York: Pantheon, 1977), p. 30; *Surveiller et punir: Naissance de la prison* (Paris: Gallimard, 1975), p. 30.

3. Friedrich Nietzsche, *On the Genealogy of Morals*, trans. Walter Kaufmann (New York: Random House, 1967), p. 87; *Zur Genealogie der Moral*, in Nietzsche, *Sämtliche Werke: Kritische Studienausgabe in 15 Einzelbänden*, ed. Giorgio Colli and Mazzino Montinari, vol. 5 (Berlin: de Gruyter, 1988), p. 325.

4. Foucault, *Discipline and Punish*, p. 30/34.

5. The relevance of the psychoanalytic understanding of the "phantasmatic" and, in particular, the view of Laplanche and Pontalis that the subject is *dissimulated* in the scene of phantasy. We might consider the various stages of progress in the *Phenomenology* as successive forms of the phantasmatic, that is, successive ways in which the subject becomes dissimulated in and as the scene of its action.

6. See Sigmund Freud, "On Narcissism: An Introduction," *The Standard Edition of the Complete Psychological Works of Sigmund Freud*,

ed. and trans. James Strachey, 24 vols. (London: Hogarth, 1953–74), 14: 73–104, for a discussion of the origins of conscience in the repression of homosexuality.

7. Here one can see that Foucault's critique of Freud in *The History of Sexuality, Volume 1* is partially wrong. Foucault's view that psychoanalysis fails to understand how law produces desire is itself a failure to understand the way in which prohibition is productive. Foucault reserves the term "power" for a productive operation that is understood not to apply to "law." Yet we see that an insurmountable equivocation between the two terms is produced once law is understood as productive.

8. Sigmund Freud, *Civilization and Its Discontents*, trans. James Strachey (New York: Norton, 1977), p. 84.

9. Nietzsche, *Zur Genealogie der Moral*, 411–12; my translation. Kaufman's equivalent is on pp. 162–63.

CHAPTER 2

1. Friedrich Nietzsche, *On the Genealogy of Morals*, trans. Walter Kaufmann (New York: Random House, 1967), p. 58; *Zur Genealogie der Moral*, in Nietzsche, *Sämtliche Werke: Kritische Studienausgabe in 15 Einzelbänden*, ed. Giorgio Colli and Mazzino Montinari, vol. 5 (Berlin: de Gruyter, 1988), p. 292.

2. Friedrich Nietzsche, *Beyond Good and Evil*, trans. Walter Kaufmann (New York: Random House, 1966), p. 25; *Jenseits von Gut und Böse*, in Nietzsche, *Sämtliche Werke: Kritische Studienausgabe in 15 Einzelbänden*, ed. Giorgio Colli and Mazzino Montinari, 5: 32.

3. Ibid., p. 29/36.

4. Sigmund Freud, "On the Mechanism of Paranoia," third section of "Psycho-Analytic Notes on an Autobiographical Account of a Case of Paranoia (Dementia Paranoides)," *The Standard Edition of the Complete Psychological Works of Sigmund Freud*, ed. and trans. James Strachey, 24 vols. (London: Hogarth, 1953–74) 12: 31.

5. Sigmund Freud, "On Narcissism: An Introduction," *Standard Edition*, 14: 73–104.

6. Sigmund Freud, *Civilization and Its Discontents*, trans. James Strachey (New York: Norton, 1977), p. 84.

CHAPTER 3

NOTE: This essay was previously published in John Rajchman, ed., *The Question of Identity* (New York: Routledge, 1995).

1. The following discussion borrows from and expands upon Chapter 1 of my *Bodies That Matter: On the Discursive Limits of "Sex"* (New York: Routledge, 1993), pp. 33–36.

2. See Sandra Bartky, *Femininity and Domination* (New York: Routledge, 1990).

3. Michel Foucault, *Discipline and Punish: The Birth of the Prison*, trans. Alan Sheridan (New York: Random House, 1979), p. 203; *Surveiller et punir: Naissance de la prison* (Paris: Gallimard, 1975), p. 202.

4. It is important to distinguish between the notion of the psyche, which includes the notion of the unconscious, and that of the subject, whose formation is conditioned by the exclusion of the unconscious.

5. For an extended and rich discussion of how norms work to subjectivate and, in particular, how norms are to be understood as transitive actions, see Pierre Macherey, "Towards a Natural History of Norms" in Timothy J. Armstrong, trans. and ed., *Michel Foucault/Philosopher* (Routledge: New York, 1992), pp. 176–91. In the same volume, for a discussion of Foucault as writing indirectly about Lacan, see Jacques-Alain Miller, "Michel Foucault and Psychoanalysis," pp. 58–63. On the problem of the dynamic relation between ethical demands and the subjectivity to which they are addressed, see the very useful comparative discussion of Foucault and Lacan in John Rajchman, *Truth and Eros: Foucault, Lacan, and the Question of Ethics* (New York: Routledge, 1991).

6. This is not to suggest that psychoanalysis is only to be represented by these two figures, although in this analysis it will be.

7. Michel Foucault, *The History of Sexuality, Volume 1: An Introduction*, tr. Robert Hurley (New York: Random House, 1978), p. 152; Foucault, *La volonte de savoir* (Paris: Gallimard, 1978), p. 200.

8. This question is raised in a different way by Charles Taylor when he asks whether there is a place for Augustinian "inwardness" in Foucault; see his "Foucault on Freedom and Truth," in David Couzens Hoy, ed., *Foucault: A Critical Reader* (New York: Blackwell, 1986), p. 99.

It is also taken up in an interesting way by William Connolly in his *The Augustinian Imperative* (Newbury Park, Calif.: Sage Press, 1993).

9. See my "Foucault and the Paradox of Bodily Inscriptions," *Journal of Philosophy* 86, no. 11 (November 1989): 257–79.

10. See discussions of the bodily ego in Freud, "The Ego and the Id," *The Standard Edition of the Complete Psychological Works of Sigmund Freud*, ed. and trans. James Strachey, 24 vols. (London: Hogarth, 1953–74), 19: 26, and in Margaret Whitford, *Luce Irigaray: Philosophy in the Feminine* (London: Routledge, 1991), pp. 53–74.

11. For a fuller explanation of Foucault's reworking of Aristotle, see "Bodies that Matter" in my *Bodies that Matter*, pp. 32–36.

12. "What was at issue was not whether the prison environment was too harsh or too aseptic, too primitive or too efficient, but its very materiality as an instrument and vector of power," *Discipline and Punish*, p. 30; *Surveiller et punir*, p. 35.

13. See Foucault, "Nietzsche, Genealogy, History," in *The Foucault Reader*, ed. Paul Rabinow (New York: Pantheon, 1984).

14. See Zakia Pathak and Rajeswari Sunder Rajan, "Shahbano," in Judith Butler and Joan Scott, eds., *Feminists Theorize the Political* (New York: Routledge, 1992), pp. 257–79.

15. Louis Althusser, "Ideology and Ideological State Apparatuses (Notes Towards an Investigation)," *Lenin and Philosophy and Other Essays*, trans. Ben Brewster (New York: Monthly Review Press, 1971), pp. 170–77.

16. For an excellent book that appropriates this Althusserian problematic for feminism, see Denise Riley, *"Am I That Name?": Feminism and the Category of 'Women' in History* (Minneapolis: University of Minnesota Press, 1988).

17. See Slavoj Žižek on the social interpellation of the proper name in *The Sublime Object of Ideology* (London: Verso, 1989), pp. 87–102.

18. Jacqueline Rose, *Sexuality in the Field of Vision* (London: Verso, 1987), pp. 90–91.

19. Foucault, *The History of Sexuality, Volume 1*, pp. 95–96.

20. Foucault, "The Subject and Power," *Michel Foucault: Beyond Structuralism and Hermeneutics*, ed. Hubert L. Dreyfus and Paul Rabinow (Chicago: University of Chicago Press, 1982), p. 212.

21. See the preface to Victor Burgin, James Donald, and Cora Kaplan, eds., *Formations of Fantasy* (London: Methuen, 1986), for a psychoanalytic warning against "collapsing" the psychic and the social.

22. In the above, the terms "attachment" and "investment" might be understood as intentional in the phenomenological sense, that is, as libidinal movements or trajectories which always take an object. There is no free-floating attachment which subsequently takes an object; rather, an attachment is always an attachment *to* an object, where that to which it is attached alters the attachment itself. The transferability of attachment presupposes that the object to which an attachment is made may change, but that the attachment will persist and will always take some object, and that this action of binding to (tied always to a certain warding off) is the constitutive action of attachment. This notion of attachment seems close to certain efforts to account for drives in non-biologistic terms (to be distinguished from efforts that take the biological seriously). Here one might seek recourse to Gilles Deleuze's reading of drives in *Masochism: An Interpretation of Coldness and Cruelty* (New York: Braziller, 1971; *Présentation de Sacher-Masoch* [Paris: Minuit, 1967]), in which he suggests that drives may be understood as the pulsionality of positing or valuation. See also Jean Laplanche's recent discussions in which "the drive" becomes indissociable from its cultural articulation: "we think it necessary to conceive of a dual expository stage: on the one hand, the preliminary stage of an organism that is bound to homeostasis and self-preservation, and, on the other hand, the stage of the adult cultural world in which the infant is immediately and completely immersed," *Jean Laplanche: Seduction, Translation, Drives*, ed. John Fletcher and Martin Stanton (London: Institute of Contemporary Arts, 1992), p. 187.

CHAPTER 4

1. See Walter Benjamin, *On the Origins of German Tragic Drama*, trans. Peter Osborne (Cambridge: MIT Press, 1987).

2. I thank Hayden White for this suggestion.

3. Nietzsche distinguishes between conscience and bad conscience

in *On the Genealogy of Morals*, linking the first with the capacity to promise and the second to the problem of internalization and of debt. The distinction appears not to be sustained, as it becomes apparent that the being who promises can only stand for his/her future by first becoming regular, that is, by internalizing the law or, to be precise, "burning it into the will." Internalization, introduced in the second essay, section 16, involves the turning of the will (or instincts) against itself. In section fifteen, Nietzsche introduces freedom as that which turns against itself in the making of bad conscience: "This *instinct for freedom* forcibly made latent . . . this instinct for freedom pushed back and repressed, incarcerated within and finally able to discharge and vent itself only on itself: that, and that alone, is what the *bad conscience* is in its beginnings" (Friedrich Nietzsche, *On the Genealogy of Morals*, trans. Walter Kaufmann and R. J. Hollingdale [New York: Random House, 1967], p. 87).

4. Louis Althusser, "Ideology and Ideological State Apparatuses (Notes Towards an Investigation)," *Lenin and Philosophy and Other Essays*, trans. Ben Brewster (New York: Monthly Review Press, 1971), pp. 127–88; "Ideologie et appareils ideologiques d'etat," *Positions* (Paris: Editions Sociales, 1976), pp. 67–126.

5. Althusser implicates his own writing in the version of ideological interpellation that he explains: "it is essential to realize that both he who is writing these lines and the reader who reads them are themselves subjects, and therefore ideological subjects (a tautological proposition, i.e. that the author and the reader of these lines both live 'spontaneously' or 'naturally' in ideology" (ibid., p. 171; p. 110). In this remark, Althusser presumes the authoritative capacities of the voice and insists that his writing, to the extent that it is ideological, addresses its reader as would a voice.

6. Ibid., p. 177.

7. See Kaja Silverman, *The Acoustic Mirror: The Female Voice in Psychoanalysis and Cinema* (Bloomington: Indiana University Press, 1988). Silverman notes the "theological" dimension of the "voice-over" in film, which always escapes the viewer's gaze (p. 49). Silverman also makes clear that the voice recognized in the cinematic presentation of voice is not only the maternal voice, but a repudiated dimension of the masculine subject's own voice (pp. 80–81). Silver-

man's analysis sheds light on the "voice" of ideology insofar as the subject who turns around already knows the voice to which he responds, suggesting an irreducible ambiguity between the "voice" of conscience and the "voice" of the law.

8. See section I in Louis Althusser, *L'avenir dure longtemps, suivi les faits* (Paris: Éditions STOCK/IMEC, 1992).

9. Louis Althusser and Étienne Balibar, *Reading Capital*, trans. Ben Brewster (London: Verso, 1970), p. 26; *Lire le Capital* (Paris: François Maspero, 1968).

10. Jean-Marie Vincent, "La lecture symptomale chez Althusser," in Futur Antérieur, ed., *Sur Althusser: Passages* (Paris: Éditions L'Harmattan, 1993), p. 97 (my translation).

11. Althusser, "Ideology and Ideological State Apparatuses," p. 132; "Ideologie," p. 72.

12. One might usefully compare Max Weber's *The Protestant Ethic* with Althusser on this point. In both, labor is effectively guaranteed through a Christian ethic, although in Althusser the religious inflection appears to be more Catholic than Protestant.

13. Pierre Bourdieu elaborates the concept of the *habitus* in *The Logic of Practice* (Stanford: Stanford University Press, 1990), pp. 66–79, where he analyzes the embodied rituals of everydayness by which a given culture produces and sustains belief in its own "obviousness." Bourdieu underscores the place of the body, its gestures, its stylistics, its unconscious "knowingness" as the site for the reconstitution of a practical sense without which social reality could not be constituted. Bourdieu's notion of the *habitus* might well be read as a reformulation of Althusser's notion of ideology. Whereas Althusser writes that ideology constitutes the "obviousness" of the subject, but that this obviousness is the effect of a *dispositif*, the same term reemerges in Bourdieu to describe the way in which a *habitus* generates certain beliefs. For Bourdieu, dispositions are generative and transposable. Note in Althusser's "Ideology and Ideological State Apparatuses" the inception of this latter reappropriation: "An individual believes in God, or Duty, or Justice, etc. This belief derives (for everyone, i.e. for all those who live in an ideological representation of ideology, which reduces ideology to ideas endowed by definition with a spiritual exis-

tence) from the ideas of the individual concerned, i.e. from him as a subject with a consciousness which contains the ideas of his belief. In this way, i.e. by means of the absolutely ideological 'conceptual' device (*dispositif*) thus set up (a subject endowed with a consciousness in which he freely forms or freely recognizes ideas in which he believes), the (material) attitude of the subject concerned naturally follows" (p. 167).

14. See Slavoj Žižek, *The Sublime Object of Ideology* (London: Verso, 1989), pp. 1–2.

15. Mladen Dolar, "Beyond Interpellation," *Qui Parle* 6, no. 2 (Spring–Summer 1993): 73–96. The English version is a revision of the original, "Jenseits der Anrufung," in Slavoj Žižek, ed., *Gestalten der Autorität* (Vienna: Hora Verlag, 1991).

16. Althusser, "Ideology and Ideological State Apparatuses," p. 166.

17. Dolar, "Beyond Interpellation," p. 76.

18. Althusser, "Ideology and Ideological State Apparatuses," pp. 169–70; "Ideologie," p. 109.

19. Dolar, "Beyond Interpellation," p. 78.

20. Giorgio Agamben, *The Coming Community*, trans. Michael Hardt (Minneapolis: University of Minnesota Press, 1993), p. 43.

CHAPTER 5

NOTE: This paper was first presented at the Division 39 Meetings of the American Psychological Association in New York City in April 1993. It was subsequently published with the replies from and to Adam Phillips in *Psychoanalytic Dialogues: A Journal of Relational Perspectives* 5 no. 2 (1995): 165–94.

1. Sigmund Freud, *The Ego and the Id*, in *The Standard Edition of the Complete Psychological Works of Sigmund Freud*, ed. and trans. James Strachey, 24 vols. (London: Hogarth, 1953–74), 19: 16.

2. Presumably, sexuality must be trained away from things, animals, parts of all of the above, and narcissistic attachments of various kinds.

3. The notion of foreclosure has become Lacanian terminology for Freud's notion of *Verwerfung*. Distinguished from repression under-

stood as an action by an already-formed subject, foreclosure is an act of negation that founds and forms the subject. See the entry "Forclusion" in J. Laplanche and J.-B. Pontalis, *Vocabulaire de la psychanalyse* (Paris: Presses Universitaires de France, 1967), pp. 163–67.

4. Sigmund Freud, "Mourning and Melancholia," *Standard Edition*, 14: 169.

5. Sigmund Freud, "On Narcissism: An Introduction," *Standard Edition*, 14: 81–82.

6. See Freud, *Civilization and Its Discontents*, trans. James Strachey, (New York: Norton, 1977), pp. 81–92.

7. See "Contagious Word: 'Homosexuality' and the Military," in my *Excitable Speech* (New York: Routledge, 1996).

8. See my *Bodies That Matter* (New York: Routledge, 1993), pp. 169–77.

9. The following argument is taken from my *Bodies That Matter*, pp. 233–36.

10. See "Freud and the Melancholia of Gender" in my *Gender Trouble: Feminism and the Subversion of Identity* (New York: Routledge, 1990).

11. This is not to suggest that an exclusionary matrix rigorously distinguishes between how one identifies and how one desires; it is quite possible to have overlapping identification and desire in heterosexual or homosexual exchange, or in a bisexual history of sexual practice. Furthermore, "masculinity" and "femininity" do not exhaust the terms for either eroticized identification or desire.

12. See Douglas Crimp, "Mourning and Militancy," *October* 51 (Winter 1989): 97–107.

13. Leo Bersani, *The Freudian Body: Psychoanalysis and Art* (New York: Columbia University Press, 1986), pp. 64–66, 112–13.

Notes to Phillips Reply

1. Freud, *The Ego and the Id*, 19: 12–59.

2. Mikkel Borch-Jacobsen, *The Emotional Tie* (Stanford: Stanford University Press, 1993); Leo Bersani, *The Freudian Body*.

3. Freud, *Three Essays on the History of Sexuality*, *Standard Edition*, 7: 125–243.

4. Freud, "Mourning and Melancholia."

5. Quoted in S. Dunn, *Walking Light* (New York: Norton, 1993).

6. Mary Douglas, *Purity and Danger* (London, Routledge, 1966).

CHAPTER 6

1. See Eric Santner, *Stranded Objects: Mourning, Memory, and Film in Postwar Germany* (Ithaca: Cornell University Press, 1990), and Alexander and Margarate Mitscherlich, *The Inability to Mourn: Principles of Collective Behavior*, trans. Beverley R. Placzek (New York: Grove Press, 1975). See also, for a feminist account that situates melancholia within the production of sexual difference, Juliana Schiesari, *The Gendering of Melancholia: Feminism, Psychoanalysis, and the Symbolics of Loss in Renaissance Literature* (Ithaca: Cornell University Press, 1992).

2. Sigmund Freud, "Mourning and Melancholia," *The Standard Edition of the Complete Psychological Works of Sigmund Freud*, ed. and trans. James Strachey, 24 vols. (London: Hogarth, 1953–74), 14: 256.

3. Here Melanie Klein's trenchant intervention on the relation of melancholia to paranoia and manic-depressive states does not carry the analysis far enough. Her theory tends to rely on tropes of internality without asking whether such tropes are the effects of a melancholia that they seek to explain. See "A Contribution to the Psychogenesis of Manic-Depressive States" (1935) and "Mourning and Its Relation to Manic-Depressive States" (1935) in *The Selected Melanie Klein*, ed. Juliet Mitchell (London: Penguin, 1986). For an excellent essay on Klein and the primary status of aggression, see Jacqueline Rose's "Negativity in the Work of Melanie Klein," in *Why War? — Psychoanalysis, Politics, and the Return to Melanie Klein* (Oxford: Basil Blackwell, 1993), pp. 137–90.

4. Here Freud replaces the term *Sachvorstellung*, used in his essay "The Unconscious" (*Standard Edition*, 14: 201), by *Dingvorstellung*. In the *Standard Edition*, James Strachey notes that *Dingvorstellung* appears in *The Interpretation of Dreams* in the discussion of jokes. The distinction is that between a word-presentation and a thing-presentation. Strachey explains that the latter consists in "the cathexis, if not of the direct memory-images of the thing, at least of remoter memory-traces derived from these" (ibid.).

5. Freud concedes as much earlier in the essay when he remarks

that "the loss of a love object is an excellent opportunity for the ambivalence in love-relationships to make itself effective and come into the open" (250–51). Toward the end of the essay, Freud remarks upon "an essential analogy between mourning and melancholia": mourning impels the ego to detach from its lost object in order to continue to live, and melancholia, through "the struggle of ambivalence loosen(s) the fixation of the libido to the object by disparaging it" (257).

6. Walter Benjamin, *The Origin of the German Tragic Drama*, trans. John Osborne (London: NLB, 1977), pp. 92–97.

7. Sigmund Freud, "Trauer und Melancholie," *Psychologie des Unbewussten, Studienausgabe* (Frankfurt a. M.: S. Fischer, 1982), 193–212.

8. See Roy Schaefer, *A New Language for Psychoanalysis* (New Haven: Yale University Press, 1976), p. 177. For a view of fantasy that operates within melancholia, see chapter one of Nicolas Abraham and Maria Torok, *The Shell and the Kernel: Renewals of Psychoanalysis*, tr. and ed. Nicholas T. Rand (Chicago: University of Chicago Press, 1994).

9. "The image of man's body is the principle of every unity he perceives in objects . . . all the objects of his world are always structured around the wandering shadow of his own ego [*l'ombre errante de son propre moi*]" (Jacques Lacan, *The Seminar of Jacques Lacan, Book II*, trans. Sylvana Tomaselli [New York: W. W. Norton, 1991], p. 166; *Le Seminaire, livre II* [Paris: Seuil, 1978], p. 198).

10. Sigmund Freud, *The Ego and the Id, The Standard Edition*, 19: 54. ("Wie kommt es nun, dass bei der Melancholie das der Ich zu einer Art Sammelstätte der Todestriebe werden kann?")

11. On primary mimesis, see Mikkel Borch-Jacobsen, *The Emotional Tie: Psychoanalysis, Mimesis, and Affect* (Stanford: Stanford University Press, 1993).

12. Homi K. Bhabha, "Postcolonial Authority and Postmodern Guilt," in Lawrence Grossberg et al., eds., *Cultural Studies: A Reader* (New York: Routledge, 1992), pp. 65–66.

13. Ibid., p. 66.

14. Freud, *The Ego and the Id*, p. 253.

15. Freud, "Mourning and Melancholia," p. 254.

16. Jessica Benjamin has argued something similar in *Bonds of Love* (New York: Pantheon, 1988), and Kaja Silverman has made the case

for "heteropathic identification" in *The Threshold of the Visible World* (New York: Routledge, 1996). Based in quite different psychoanalytic views, each has contested the centrality of incorporation and super-egoic functions in the account of internalization.

17. Jacques Derrida, remarks, Humanities Research Institute, University of California, Irvine, April 5, 1995.

Index